To Bob Novote:

Best wishes for Keep voting
the 12g varieties

Bob Brown

Industrial Problem Solving

Isolating the Key Variables

Robert W. Traver

Hitchcock Publishing Co.
Carol Stream, Illinois 60188

Library of Congress Catalog Number 89-81794

Traver, Robert W.
Industrial Problem Solving: Isolating the Key Variables

First Edition
©1989 by Hitchcock Publishing Co., Carol Stream, IL 60188
A Capital Cities/ABC Inc. company
Loren M. Walsh, President

Printed in the United States of America

10 9 8 7 6 5 4 3 2 1

∞This book has been printed on high quality, low glare, acid free paper.

ISBN 0-933931-13-1

Margot Goldsmith: Editor
Jeannette Colfer: Word Processing
Annette Mola: Composing
Arlene Bartolini: Production Coordinator
Charles Doyle, Bev Morris, Mary Pacentine, Joan Wilder: Production
Jean McNamara: Art Director
Steve Falco: Cover Design
Raymond J. Kimber: Director, Book Publishing

ii

Preface

With the increasing emphasis on quality in American industry, numerous books have been written on many aspects of product and service quality. Some of these books focus on statistical process control and/or statistical concepts, while many others emphasize the importance of senior management commitment, involvement, participation and support. This emphasis on senior management commitment is sound, because without it quality programs would prove unsuccessful or at best short lived. Many of these management-oriented books also stress quality systems—which mean open-ended and ongoing processes, rather than closed-ended programs.

Industrial Problem Solving: Isolating the Key Variables stresses problem solving as a system for continuous improvement and does not merely present statistical concepts or describe statistical process control (SPC). The book emphasizes the use of graphical analysis in problem solving because it is straightforward and far easier to understand and implement than complex statistical methods.

Graphical analysis is at the heart of the multi-vari problem-solving strategy of key variable isolation, which is the focus of the book. Multi-vari identifies which variables and/or interactions are causing quality problems and then guides the elimination of the problem and control of the variables. Production then becomes more consistent and less sensitive to outside influences.

From the 1950's through the early 1970's a group of management consultants under Dorian Shainin at Rath & Strong, Inc., used this problem-solving strategy under the name *statistical engineering* to solve engineering and manufacturing problems. After a time this title was replaced by the term *variation research*. Later, I felt that the word research could be misleading so I modified the term to *variables isolation*. It seemed an apt title because the task is always to isolate the variable(s) or interaction of variables that causes problems.

The problem-solving strategy of what I now call *key variable isolation* is not a fancy name for statistical methods nor is it an alternative to classical statistical methods. Instead, it incorporates these techniques when they are appropriate. Key variable isolation has its own set of methods and procedures.

An important element of key variable isolation is the multi-vari study, which reveals clues to the cause of the problem. Although different names can be attached to some specific techniques, the real strength of key variable isolation lies in the integration of old and new methods into a realistic problem-solving strategy.

Anyone involved in reducing product variation, improving consistency and reducing the incidence of defective products and the related costs of poor quality will benefit from this book. In particular, process, manufacturing, product, industrial and quality control/ assurance engineers should find the concepts important and useful. All management in the manufacturing sector should also become familiar with the key variable isolation strategy so that they can recognize situations where its application would be beneficial.

Using key variable isolation as the way to locate the key variable(s) goes a long way toward realizing Walter Shewhart's classic statement, "The long-range contribution of statistics depends not so much upon getting a lot of highly trained statisticians into industry, as it does in creating a statistically minded generation of physicists, chemists, engineers, and others who will . . . have a hand in developing and directing the production processes of tomorrow." Perhaps even more to the point: employees do not have to become statisticians— they need to learn how to apply basic statistical concepts as tools to solve industrial problems.

Five of my associates at Reddy, Rosen, Traver & Woods, Inc., have each contributed a chapter to this book to ensure that a broad range of industries would be covered. I am grateful to them for their input and support.

Robert W. Traver

Foreword

Everyone talks about industrial problem solving and some books explain how to do it. These books typically provide precise methods for selecting the problem to work on and ways to protect customers from receiving defective products. The instructions often are to not treat the symptoms, but to define the root cause so that the real problem can be corrected. It sounds so simple. All you have to do is define the root cause—but these books never tell you how. Why do they avoid giving details about this crucial activity? The reason is simple. Defining the root cause is very difficult and complex, and they don't have a good way of finding the cause that works all the time.

There are a number of ways to get to the root of an industrial problem. A good failure analysis laboratory can provide the insight necessary to understand how a failure such as a broken bolt occurred. Duplicating the failure under laboratory conditions also has proven an effective way to define the root cause of problems. Each of these approaches works well, but they require expensive laboratories and highly trained personnel.

Excessive variation is at the heart of most problems, at least the difficult ones. Variation is part of life. No two items or acts are exactly identical. Even identical twins have very different fingerprints, voice patterns and personal values. No two screws made on the same machine are exactly the same. Equipment may not be sensitive enough to measure the variation, but it exists. Some variation is good. It keeps our lives from being monotonous. No one would like steak, mashed potatoes and peas three times a day, every day of the week. They are good for a special treat, but would get old and boring if eaten at every meal.

Some variation—within specific limits—has little or no effect on output. In other cases, variation can cause an entire plant to come to a halt. The variation we're concerned about here is the variation that causes problems resulting in waste. There is no such thing as a random problem, just problems whose occurrence is more or less infrequent—meaning that the combination of specific variables occurs more or less infrequently. The art of defining the root cause is the art of variables analysis and isolation.

The root cause of a problem has been found when the key variables that caused the problem have been isolated. Over the years, there have been many methods developed to isolate key variables. Designed experiments and Taguchi methods are popular today. But the difficulties and effort required to prepare and conduct these studies cause them to be used on only a small fraction of the problems. Engineers, managers, production employees and sales personnel solve most of their problems by brute force and a lot of luck. Even then, most of the time the answer that is implemented is not the best solution to the problem.

At last, a simple but effective way of systematically looking at and understanding variation has been developed—key variable isolation using multi-vari. This technique unlocks the door and shows users how to interpret the clues that solve even the most difficult problems. Key variable isolation using multi-vari provides a systematic approach that can be used to unlock the mysteries of variation. By studying different types of variation, the source of the variation can be identified. Then, the problem solver can quickly and effectively reduce the many potential sources to a critical few and often to a single factor, thereby greatly simplifying the problem evaluation cycle and reducing the amount of data that needs to be collected.

The results can be outstanding:

- Problems can be solved faster
- Fewer samples are required
- Less-skilled people can solve very complex problems
- Preventive and corrective action plans can be evaluated quickly
- Non-technical people can easily understand the results of a technical evaluation.

The techniques defined in this book are not new and untried. They are based on more than three decades of successful practical experience by a group of highly skilled consultants and their clients. The book is particularly helpful because it presents theory and then provides detailed case studies that describe exactly how the theory is applied. The presentation of this valuable material is enhanced by the wealth of knowledge and practical experience that Robert Traver and his associates have accumulated throughout the years.

H. James Harrington

INTRODUCTION

Designed experiments and other statistical concepts have been making a positive contribution to American industry for many decades. However, the applications of these concepts during this time have differed greatly in various industries and even within the same company. Unfortunately, the gap between theory and the actual application of these concepts on the factory floor has often remained too wide.

In contrast to highly structured statistical techniques, key variable isolation interweaves engineering, manufacturing and statistical work so tightly that precise delineation is not possible. Investigative procedures such as detective work and key variable isolation contain both deductive and inductive aspects. One can learn the deductive aspects of detective work, such as fingerprinting or ballistics, from a book. Inductive skills, however, are much more difficult to acquire, and practice is needed to learn how to leap from clues to conclusion. Inductive skills may not be documentable or even teachable and thus it may not be possible to write a recipe approach to either detective work or key variable isolation. It is possible, however, to explain the strategy and methods behind key variable isolation and to illustrate these methods with a series of case studies. This approach enables problem solvers to begin to acquire the skills necessary to use key variable isolation and to understand the wide range of the method's applicability.

In every industry in which these techniques have been introduced, some people initially doubted that the consultants and their programs could help because, "These outsiders don't understand our problems." But key variable isolation programs are always joint programs in which the consultants work very closely with the client's technical people. Key variable isolation utilizes the technical knowledge in each industry because the consultants cannot apply these strategies in a vacuum. They depend on specific technical input from the client's technical personnel. Effective practitioners of key variable isolation draw on this technical expertise to help determine ways to quantify product defectiveness if no numerical scale exists; to design the tests; to iron out the problems of how to run tests; and to interpret the meaning of the data and conclusions. It is the insightful evaluation of the patterns of variation in the data that allows problem solvers to leap ahead to the next step using inductive reasoning. Key variable isolation techniques do not replace engineering judgment and manufacturing know-how—they enhance them. The engineer who has learned to use the key variable isolation tools becomes far more effective and valuable.

While every company is unique, problems are not. The advantage of the key variable isolation view of manufacturing problems is that the strategy can be applied to any industrial situation. Each problem is viewed from the standpoint of patterns of variation, and each successive test brings the investigator closer to the solution.

Acknowledgement

It was only through the patient editing by my daughter, Elizabeth Traver, that a mass of jottings was converted into a readable book.

Dedication

This book is dedicated to Valarie, my wife, for her cheerful typing of the many revisions of the material and the plotting and replotting of the numerous figures.

Contents

Industrial Problem Solving

Isolating the Key Variables

CHAPTER 1

Key Variable Isolation

All manufacturing processes vary and, as a result, the products made by those processes also vary. Generally, product variation within specified limits is considered normal and acceptable. But sometimes the physical dimensions, performance characteristics or visual appearance of a product will exceed the allowable limits; such product is often referred to as being defective*. The goal of modern manufacturing is to prevent defective products from being made in the first place. In real life, however, defective products are occasionally made, even by processes that have been running a long time and from which all the "bugs" were thought to have been removed.

It is generally accepted that product defects are caused by one or more process input variables that are not performing properly. In this book, the term **key variable** (or key **process** variable) will refer to the process input variable(s) that must be corrected or adjusted before the product made by the process can meet all the specified requirements. Process input variables, such as mold temperature, machine speed, raw material composition, air pressure, operator techniques and others become key variables when they cause or

---

*In this book the term defective will be applied to product that does not meet specified requirements in one or more ways. Generally, the distinction will not be made as to whether such product is "fit to use," or whether it can be reworked or salvaged.

contribute to product problems.

Modern companies use many sources of information in order to determine whether there are problems in their products. Among the more common outside sources are customer complaints, warranty claims and salesmen's reports. Inside sources might include total quality assurance audits, quality control studies including Shewhart X-bar and R charts, excessive scrap and rework rates and others. However, in most cases determining that there is a problem is the easiest part. The hard part is to determine what is causing the problem. In this book the techniques for determining the cause of product problems are referred to as **key variable isolation**. Key variable isolation is the series of techniques used to determine which process variables contribute to or are responsible for defective product.

Key variable isolation does not make prior assumptions as to which process variable(s) is (are) responsible for problems in manufactured product. Instead, key variable isolation usually begins by sampling and inspecting the products being produced by the process. The results of the inspection are then graphed, plotted or otherwise analyzed using a technique called a multi-vari study. This analysis of the data inevitably rules out some process variables as the causes of product problems and often suggests other process variables. The step-by-step identification of types or patterns of variation is used to progressively reduce the field of process variables that might be causing the problem. Ultimately, only those process variables that are likely to be the source of the problem will remain to be studied.

Comparing Approaches

The traditional engineering approach to problem solving provides solutions to many quality problems. This approach involves the following steps:

1. Observe
2. Think
3. Try
4. Explain.

Using these steps, an industrial investigator—when confronted with a manufacturing quality problem such as a physical defect or an out-of-tolerance dimension—will first observe the problem. Then, the investigator will think of what process variable might be causing the problem. For example, the cause might seem to be that the pressure is too high, the temperature is too low, the time is too long, the coolant is not right or the raw material is out of specification. The investigator next will try something such as adjusting the process variable thought to be the cause of the problem to see if that will solve the problem. If the problem seems to disappear, the investigator might explain the solution as follows: the temperature was too low; the temperature was then increased and now the process works properly.

Some quality problems of a general nature can be resolved simply by involving the workers. Brainstorming can also be useful in solving problems. However, when a difficult problem does not yield to the traditional engineering approach, employee involvement or brainstorming, management may:

- Purchase more expensive manufacturing equipment
- Select a different method of manufacturing
- Eliminate the product from the product line
- Accept the reduced quality
- Design around the problem.

All of these options are costly and usually are chosen because the real cause of the product problem—that is, the key process variable (or variables)—has not been identified. Key variable isolation is one way to approach apparently unsolvable problems. Key process variable isolation using multi-vari, which yields a rapid convergence toward problem solution, is a systematic way of "listening" to a manufacturing process.

The power and efficiency of the key variable isolation approach lie in its capacity to frame or bracket different, important aspects of a complete manufacturing process and its product. This framing or bracketing often results in an elimination of one or more process variables that were previously thought to have a major impact on the product but are then found to have insignificant influence. Thus, the industrial investigator can focus on the aspects of the manufacturing operation that are most likely to be responsible for product problems.

Key variable isolation may be characterized as:

1. A form of industrial detective work in which the investigator asks open-ended questions about the product and the process

2. A strategy using unusual combinations of statistical methods

3. The application of statistical methods, engineering judgment, manufacturing know-how and common sense to solve the problem at hand.

Key variable isolation uses techniques such as multi-vari analysis and designed experimentation along with numerical rating scales, measles charts, overstress testing, component search, variables search and other analytic methods to determine the cause of product problems.

Learning the Methods

Key variable isolation is best learned through training under the "internship" method. A number of years ago a study determined the factors that produced the best surgeons. The study concluded that the only significant factor was the amount of time the prospective surgeon spent under the watchful eye and careful guidance of a successful surgeon acting as a coach, i.e., through internship. While it is true that people do learn from their mistakes, they learn far more rapidly and efficiently by doing things right the first time. The experienced practitioner contributes to the learning process by coaching the proper methods.

Key variable isolation may be taught in a classroom situation. Solving real-life problems, however, requires a major leap from classroom training. Therefore, in addition to theory, case histories may be presented to help personnel understand how key variable isolation has actually been used. People often find that their specific problems are similar to those presented in a case history and can better learn by comparing the two situations.

After the case histories have been studied, trainees may be given hypothetical situations and asked to solve problems for which there may be a number of solutions. Typically, the classroom is divided into teams of three to five people for this problem-solving exercise. In a larger class the problems may be assigned to more than one team. Appendices 1 and 2 present two hypothetical situations, followed by their solutions, that can be used to introduce the concepts of key variable isolation to company personnel.

CHAPTER 2

Multi-Vari Studies

The multi-vari technique is an integral part of the key variable isolation strategy. Using multi-vari helps the industrial investigator to efficiently narrow the field of process input variables that may be causing problems in a product.

Multi-vari begins with a stratified sampling and inspection of products being produced by the manufacturing process. The inspection results are then graphed, plotted or otherwise analyzed. From a systematic analysis of the inspection results the investigator can determine the patterns of variation that are occurring in the process. A study might reveal, for example, that significant variation is occurring from shift to shift in a plastic injection molding operation; pieces produced during the first shift are greatly different from pieces produced during the second shift. This information allows the investigator to focus attention on the process input variables that can cause such variation. At the same time, the investigator can eliminate from consideration any variable that could not cause shift-to-shift variation. In this way, the investigator ultimately can identify the variable(s) that are causing the product problem (i.e., the investigator can isolate the *key* variable or variables). For example, if the same bag of plastic raw material was used during both shifts of the plastic injection molding operation it is unlikely that raw material composition is the key variable. If, however, a new lot of raw material was started at the beginning of the second shift, raw material composition could well be the key process variable.

The multi-vari technique may seem elementary, but is in fact a powerful tool. Many industrial problems go unsolved for long periods of time because in the "Think" step of the traditional engineering approach an incorrect assumption leads the investigation in the wrong direction. In multi-vari, however, the investigation is confined to process variables that fit the clues.

Types of Variation

Figures 1, 2 and 3 present three multi-vari charts that illustrate common types of variation that can occur in the product: within-piece variation, piece-to-piece variation and time-to-time variation. (Other types of variation, such as side-to-side, operator-to-operator, machine-to-machine, cycle-to-cycle, day-to-day, etc., exist in industry but will not be discussed in this chapter.) The figures are derived from hypothetical operating processes that are making mostly good product. For the purposes of these three figures, assume that measurements were made at two places on the same feature of each piece (as shown in Figure 4), and the sampling of pieces was done in groups of five.

■ Figure 1 shows significant within-piece variation—measurements made at two different places on the same feature of the same piece vary as much as seven "points" (2 to 9 on piece number 4. This variation is highlighted by a double dotted line). There is little piece-to-piece variation—only pieces 36 and 73 show as much as a 1 "point" difference from the average of the other pieces. The time-to-time variation—from one group of five pieces to the next, each group taken at a different time—is also insignificant. This pattern suggests that whatever process variable is causing the variation is causing it within the piece. Suppose that Figure 1 reflects a machining process that was used to make a cylindrical part such as automobile engine piston pins. Excessive within-piece variation would indicate that individual pin diameters are not consistent from one end of the pin to the other.

■ Figure 2 shows significant piece-to-piece variation (highlighted by a double dotted line). The piece-to-piece variation is as much as 5 "points" (piece number 2 to piece number 3). Within-piece variation, however, is slight—about 1 to 2 "points" on all pieces. Likewise, the variation from time to time is small; that is, the average of the measurements of the first group of five pieces is similar to the averages of the second and third group, even though the samples were taken at different times. This pattern indicates that the variation is caused by one or more process variables that vary excessively from piece to piece.

■ Figure 3 shows major time-to-time variation, ranging on the measurement scale from about 13 for the first group of five pieces to 4 for the second group (the double dotted line used to highlight the time-to-time variation extends from the average of the first group of pieces to the average of the second group of pieces). The within-piece variation is small—most pieces vary less than 1 "point"(pieces 3, 37,

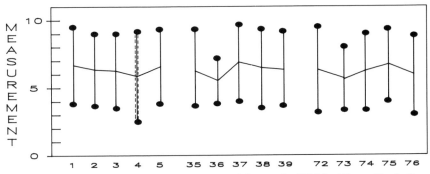

Figure 1. Within-Piece Variation

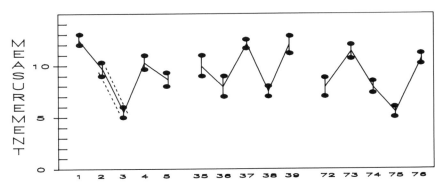

Figure 2. Piece-to-Piece Variation

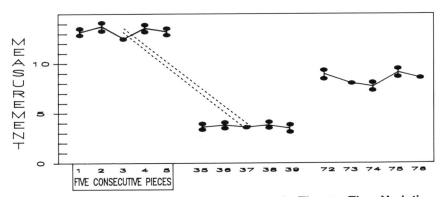

Figure 3. Time-to-Time Variation

73, and 76 have no measurable within-piece variation and are therefore plotted as a single point). The piece-to-piece variation is also slight. Thus, the major variation seems to be caused by process variables that vary excessively over time.

The next step after the initial multi-vari analysis would be to determine which variables fit the clues.

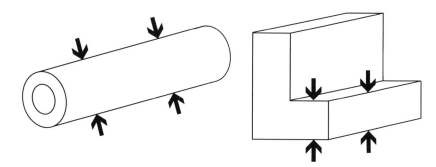

Figure 4. Examples of Two Measurements Made on the Same Feature of the Same Piece

Using the Clues

Using the multi-vari technique to identify the process variables that are most likely to be causing product problems may be compared to playing the game of 20 Questions. This game starts with one person thinking of some physical thing. Another person then has 20 questions to determine what that thing is. The first question is whether the item is animal, vegetable or mineral. If the answer is animal, two-thirds of the "universe" has been ruled out. The questioner then asks a further narrowing question such as, does it have four legs? If the answer is yes, humans, birds, fish and insects are ruled out, and the search is confined to a four-legged animal. The next question would not be whether it is a kangaroo, giraffe or panda, but rather a narrowing question such as, is it bigger than a dog? If it is not bigger than a dog, the search is further restricted to a small, four-legged animal. The game continues with questions asked that further reduce the field of possible answers.

Both 20 Questions and key variable isolation using multi-vari work in this narrowing fashion. This approach contrasts sharply with the method of continuing to guess randomly at the answer. The continued guessing method might be compared to learning in 20 Questions that the item had been narrowed down to a four-legged animal, smaller than a dog, then guessing chrysanthemum. The answer, however, cannot be chrysanthemum because it does not fit the clues. Using the multi-vari technique, the investigator can set aside the investigation of those process variables that are not likely to be causing problems and concentrate on those that are most likely to be key variables.

Multi-Vari versus Designed Experiments

It is important here to understand the difference between the multi-vari technique and the technique known as designed or factorial experiments, another method of locating the key variable(s). In a multi-vari study, the manufacturing process is intentionally not disturbed. A stratified sample is selected from an ongoing process to represent what happens during regular production without interrupting that process; that is, products manufactured during a multi-vari study are the same as products made when a study is not being run.

In a designed experiment, on the other hand, an investigator creates a special experiment in which process input variables are intentionally adjusted either individually or in combinations in order to determine which variables may be causing the problem. Multi-vari studies may be used on their own or in conjunction with designed experiments. For example, through a multi-vari study, an investigator may narrow down to three the process variables suspected of causing product problems. The investigator then might design a specific type of experiment to test the three variables and determine which of the three is the key variable.

CHAPTER 3

Quantification: The Initial Diagnostic Step

Many manufacturing problems go unsolved for long periods of time because investigators choose the wrong method of quantifying characteristics of the product. While product characteristics such as physical dimensions, electrical resistance and voltage, weight and the like are by their nature quantified, a crucial part of the problem-solving process lies in choosing which characteristics should be measured and evaluated. Most manufactured items have several or even dozens of dimensional characteristics or features that could be measured. Making and evaluating measurements on more than one or two characteristics of a product can quickly become overwhelming. Generally, however, every manufactured product possesses one (or two) major features or characteristics that appropriately reflect the results of changes or adjustments to the process. Ford Motor Co., for example, in its Q101 *Quality System Standard*, refers to such features as control characteristics. *It should be noted that in industry the word* variables *is often applied to discussions of dimensional measurements made on features or characteristics of manufactured items. In this book, however, to avoid confusion the word variables will only be used to refer to process variables (such as temperature, pressure, etc.), and not to measurements made on products.*

Product problems may also involve defects in characteristics that are visual, workmanship or cosmetic rather than dimensional in nature. Visual, workmanship and cosmetic characteristics are designated as *attributes* and are typically rated only "good" or "bad," "acceptable" or "unacceptable," "satisfactory" or "unsatisfactory." These attribute ratings, however, are not sensitive enough for problem-solving efforts. When a problem-solving effort involves the evaluation of attributes the industrial investigator must first develop a numerical scale for measuring them. As Lord Kelvin advised more than 100 years ago: "When you can measure what you're speaking about and express it in numbers, you know something about it, but when you can not measure it, when you can not express it in numbers, your knowledge is of a meagre and unsatisfactory kind." Even today many companies have not learned that lesson well enough. Lord Kelvin's advice means that, "You can't make what you can't measure because you don't know when you've got it made."

Quantifying Attributes

The following example illustrates the importance of quantifying visual or physical defects. The engineers of a company were having trouble with a particular defect while producing a laminated plastic product. They would run a number of units one way and count the percent defective, then run a number of units another way and count that percent defective. Percent defective calculations, however, do not consider the degree of defectiveness. After struggling with the process improvement project the problem-solving team replaced the percent defective method with a numerical rating scale shown in Figure 5. This scale uses numbers 0 to 5 to evaluate the product. Note that nothing in this numerical scale states whether the product is acceptable. The scale simply provides a rating that can be used for determining changes in the manufacturing process. The objective of creating such a scale was to solve the defect problem, not to decide whether to ship the product.

```
0 - PERFECT.
1 - VERY FAINT--INCIPIENT, USUALLY NEAR A CORNER.
2 - DEFINITELY SHOWING--BUT LESS THAN THE AVERAGE
      SEEN DURING AN EPIDEMIC.
3 - AVERAGE SEEN WHEN DEFECTS ARE OCCURRING.
      OFTEN GOING COMPLETELY ACROSS THE PRODUCT,
      MODERATELY SEVERE.
4 - HEAVY INVOLVEMENT--TYPICALLY COVERING ENTIRE
      PRODUCT, BLOTCHY, BUT NOT A SOLID MASS.
5 - AS BAD AS IT EVER GETS--TOTAL INVOLVEMENT.
```

Figure 5. Numerical Rating Scale

Companies may, however, devise other formats that combine attribute rating scales with product acceptability information. Figure 6 is an example of such a scale. The scale starts at 0, which is perfect, and goes up to 8, which denotes a very severe defect. These numerical ratings are used during process improvement projects. The

GREEN	0	PERFECT
GREEN	1	NEARLY PERFECT
GREEN	2	TOP COMMERCIAL
YELLOW	3	GOOD COMMERCIAL
YELLOW	4	FAIR COMMERCIAL
RED	5	POOR COMMERCIAL
RED	6	MAJOR DEFECT
RED	7	SEVERE DEFECT
RED	8	VERY SEVERE DEFECT

Figure 6. Numerical Rating Scale with Acceptance Guide

left-hand column of Figure 6 denotes product acceptability levels. A company might be able to ship product rated 0 to 4 (ship on "green" or "yellow") to some customers, while other customers might accept only product rated 0 to 2 (ship on "green" only). In Figure 6, a "red" identification means the product is not acceptable for shipment to any customer.

A numerical rating scale such as that shown in Figure 6 provides consistent quantification so that a company will not make the mistake of shipping an unacceptable product and perhaps lose a customer. Such a scale creates a visual gage so that all inspectors evaluate the product in the same way. The numerical score reflects the overall appearance of the product, rather than individual defects of the product; the size, combination, pattern and placement of defects are all important factors in determining the score. However, because there will always be a certain amount of subjectivity in viewing the product, the score will also be somewhat subjective. Therefore, each attribute rating system should be backed up by prominently displayed visual samples of each defect level.

Panel of Experts

To develop scales such as those shown in Figures 5 and 6, usually a panel of experts is assembled to look at samples of the product and come to a consensus. A consensus means that all persons involved agree on the figures, which then become the standard. On many of the samples the experts will agree on the score. However, there are usually some samples about which there is a disagreement. After assigning scores to those samples on which there is agreement, the panel returns to those about which there were disagreements and reviews them until agreement is reached. Once the scale has been established, other people who will be judging the product—such as the foreman, the general foreman and the operators—are brought in and their vision is "calibrated."

An example of how a panel might work toward consensus follows. An investigator was working on a visual standard program involving 11 panel members who included operators, inspectors, manufacturing supervisors and quality control personnel. The panel had finally obtained agreement on all but one sample. One inspector insisted the sample was a 3, while most of the others said it was a 2. A few panel members began by insisting the sample was a 3 but were convinced during the discussion that it was a 2. The inspector remained firm that it was a 3. In exasperation, the superintendent pointed at him and blurted, "you are overruled." The investigator quickly countered that there was no overruling in consensus programs. Finally, a quality engineer suggested that the product be buffed for a better look. One of the operators brought the product out to the shop floor, buffed it and returned to the panel. The buffing highlighted the defects and when everyone examined the product again, they all agreed that the sample was a 3. At times, "refining" needs to be done to the sample before all agree, but this is what is involved in a consensus decision.

In addition, vision needs to be "recalibrated" periodically because visual impressions are always subjective and may shift over time. Some inspectors become less careful and their scores get looser, while others become more careful, even nitpicking. Certain inspectors may even reach the point where they feel they should reject anything made in the plant. Also, during the last two or three days of the month inspectors' vision may change drastically, as they face the end-of-the-month schedule. A formal quantification system reduces or eliminates these inconsistencies.

CHAPTER 4

The Case of Out-of-Specification Coil Resistance

The following case history describes how a multi-vari study solved a long-standing problem at a company where transformers were a major product.

Coils of wire are the basic components of transformers, and one measure of how accurately the transformer coils have been wound is the electrical resistance of the wire in the coils.

The company made transformer coils on a 12-headed coil winding machine. After the coils were wound they were sent through a series of processes in order to make transformers and finally the coil resistance was measured. Occasionally, a transformer coil would be out of specification. The chief engineer of the company asked an industrial investigator to determine the cause of the problem. During the initial discussion the engineer offered some ideas such as, "The power company has voltage surges that affect this operation." He also stated that, "At the end of the day, when we run second shift, the power changes from mostly industrial and commercial to mostly residential." After the chief engineer had described these and other process input variables, all of which were electrical, the investigator decided to start the investigation by running a multi-vari study.*

---

*There are many ways to approach process problem-solving efforts. Some investigators begin by generating Shewhart X-bar and R charts, which are among the most powerful analysis tools available. But in many cases, such as this one, an initial evaluation using multi-vari can be much simpler, faster and more direct. In many cases, such as this one, the X-bar and R chart could effectively be used for process monitoring once the cause of the problem has been discovered and corrected.

To begin the study the quality control manager and the investigator collected five consecutive coils, at each of three times during one day, from each of the 12 winding heads and brought the coils directly to the resistance measuring equipment.

Evaluating the Data

Figure 7 shows coil resistances from three of the 12 heads (numbers 4, 7 and 8). A small percentage of the coils was above specification and the multi-vari study clearly shows that the problem was an incorrectly adjusted head. Head number 8 was set too close to the high limit; the coil resistances were not centered on the nominal (target) value. Many of the coils from head number 8 were within specification, but some (identified by squares in Figure 7) were over the limit. On any given head, the coil-to-coil variation was small. The time-to-time variation was also negligible and there was essentially no change between the first and second shift. After analyzing the multi-

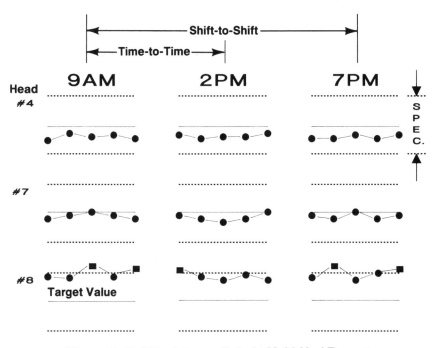

Figure 7. Coil Resistance Data in Multi-Vari Format

vari study, the investigator decided that the corrective action should be to adjust head number 8 so that the coil resistances were centered on the target value, routinely draw a sample from each head, and, if necessary readjust the process (the individual head) so that the coil resistances were centered on the nominal value.

Additional Benefits

The multi-vari study had an additional result besides correction of the problem. The study showed that variation from one coil to another (on the same head) and from time-to-time was very small. This meant that once the heads were set correctly and monitored periodically there would be even less variation than the specification allowed. Thus, the company could build to a tighter specification than had existed.' The company then had the opportunity of charging a higher price for a premium product and/or trying to reach a select segment of the market. In this situation, the solution to the problem meant more than 100 percent good product; it meant a potentially new market for the company.

The important point to recognize in this case is that the product was used to lead the investigator to the solution. The multi-vari results quickly revealed what was not causing the problem, and that knowledge narrowed the field of investigation. The problem was not solved by the traditional engineering approach of trying to guess the answer. The chief engineer had tried this approach—had, in effect, tried to "tell" the process what was wrong. The engineer thought that the problem was electrical when actually it was mechanical. Using multi-vari studies, investigators let the process do the talking and then listen to the process.

CHAPTER 5

Interactions

The cause of a manufacturing problem is often more complex than one or two key variables acting independently. Sometimes two or more process variables act together to produce a result different from that of either (or both) variables acting alone. This combined result is called an **interaction**. An everyday example of an interaction is sodium chloride or table salt. Either sodium or chlorine by itself would act as a deadly poison if swallowed. When sodium and chlorine interact, however, they produce table salt—a "result" very much different from either sodium or chlorine acting alone.

Figure 8 shows a typical interaction between two industrial process variables—temperature and pressure. A scenario involving these variables might be as follows: an engineer is concerned about the effect of the two variables in one of the company's processes when they are at their high and low limits. He decides to run a test, holding everything constant except the one variable being tested. Therefore, he performs his first test holding temperature constant at the high level while he sets the pressure at the low level. He gets a result of 5. Then he raises the pressure to the high level and gets a result of 11. The engineer returns to his office and writes in his logbook, "When I raise the pressure from the low level to the high level the output goes up." A valid conclusion.

The next day the engineer decides to verify his results. He returns to the shop floor and again holds the temperature constant, but this time at the low level. He adjusts the pressure to the low level and gets a result of 9. Then he adjusts the pressure to the high level and gets a result of 4. This time the engineer notes in his logbook: "As I raise the pressure from the low level to the high level the output goes down. Yesterday it went up. I know what the problem is—poor supervision and apathetic operators." The cause of the problem, however, is not

PRESSURE (psi)

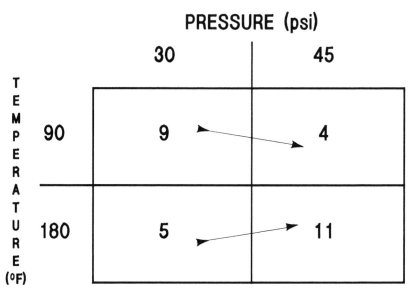

Figure 8a. Data Format

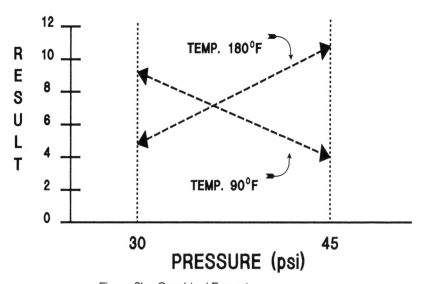

Figure 8b. Graphical Format

Figure 8. Two Ways of Showing the Results of Tests Involving Interactions

poor supervision and apathetic operators. The cause of the problem is an interaction between temperature and pressure. Interactions are common in manufacturing processes.

To describe an interaction the word *depends* must be used. In the previous example, to describe the effect of adjusting the pressure one must say, "The result depends on the temperature at which the test is run." Or, to describe the effect of adjusting the temperature one must say, "The result depends on the pressure at which the test is run." Since the engineer is unaware of the effects of interactions, he may not find them by running tests in which only one process variable is adjusted or changed while everything else is held constant. Other testing methods may be required to detect the effects of interaction.

While multi-vari analysis is usually the first choice in key variable isolation, interactions can confuse the results because multi-vari testing is intentionally performed without correcting or adjusting process input variables. To identify interactions, process variables must intentionally be adjusted in appropriate combinations and sequences. There are a number of techniques that can be used to evaluate interactions; of these, designed (or factorial) experiments probably have the longest history of use in industry.

CHAPTER 6

The Case of the Flat Beer
By John M. Reddy

Some years ago most breweries decided to switch to aluminum cans. These breweries then experienced a new quality problem unique to aluminum—leaks that seemed to be caused by small pieces of aluminum oxide called "stringers" at the rim of the cans. While no spillage of liquid occurred, on occasion the carbon dioxide in the beer would escape and in some rare instances the customer received a can of flat beer. Since the incidence of flat beer was only 60 per million cans, or 0.006 percent, virtually all breweries accepted this apparently trivial quality problem. Most executives in the brewing industry at that time decided that the cost savings realized by the use of aluminum more than compensated for the slight deterioration in quality. The cost/quality trade-off reasoning, however, was not acceptable to one brewer. This company insisted on high quality throughout the entire process. Knowingly sending out defective product was inconsistent with company policies and could not be tolerated. The company, therefore, decided to assemble a problem-solving team in order to determine the cause of the problem.

Planning the Problem-Solving Approach

A designed experiment to evaluate a problem level as small as 60 parts per million would have been too large and unwieldy to be practical. Thus, the problem-solving team decided to use an approach that involved forcing or aggravating manufacturing conditions in order to obtain data that would highlight variation from one operating condition to another. To accomplish this goal, the team decided to obtain a large sample of cans with stringers to feed into the stations where the cans were filled with beer and sealed. A month of searching by dozens of people in the company's canmaking department provided the team with 240 examples of oxide stringers in the rim area of unfilled cans.

While the actual cost of the search for these cans was small, the psychological benefits of including many people in the problem-solving process were great. Excitement built as the word passed through the company that the problem-solving team was coming to grips with a stubborn process problem. Difficult steps can often produce positive results as they did in this case: the actual cost was slight but many people gained a sense of accomplishment in attacking a supposedly impossible problem.

Setting up the Experiment

Quantification is a prerequisite for this type of study, and the team used the straightforward approach of dividing the 240 cans into three grades of 80 each. In grade 1 the oxide stringers were about 1/64 in. long; in grade 2, they ranged around 1/32 in.; and in grade 3 they were about 1/16 in. long. Piece-to-piece identification was achieved by placing one colored, indelible dot on the can just below the stringer for grade 1, two dots for grade 2 and three dots for grade 3. By placing the dots in this way, the team could tell the exact location of the stringer during the entire process. In several cases the location of the stringer provided important clues for identifying the key variables.

The team then turned its attention to the filling/sealing process. Each of the four filling/sealing stations consisted of 24 separate heads. This is analogous to 24 different "machines" ganged together on one base. Since each head was a unique "machine," the team agreed that it had to know which head filled and sealed which can. The normal production records showed leakage rates* for each station but not for each head. Control charts indicated that some stations at times produced more defects than other stations. However, there seemed to be no way to identify which head within each station

---

*The leakage rates for each of the four stations were determined as follows: As a routine test, individual filled and sealed cans were randomly selected from each station and placed in a test device. This device was able to detect and measure the rate at which carbon dioxide escaped from the can. The rate was measured in parts per million of carbon dioxide per unit of time. When the rate of leakage exceeded a specified limit, the can was considered defective, i.e., that product item was defective. If the rate of carbon dioxide leakage were very high, enough carbon dioxide could escape to result in a "flat" can of beer by the time a consumer attempted to consume it.

produced what percentage of defective product. For the experiment, the team found a way to make a small mark on each can going through head number 1. Identifying the cans filled by a specific head could then be done easily because the cans were fed into a conveyor in which the order of filling and sealing was strictly maintained.

The team judged that measuring head-to-head rather than station-to-station variation[†] would probably yield more information because past production records showed that the station-to-station variation was not great enough to identify the cause of the problem over the long term. The underlying principle involved in this decision was that problem solving usually involves delving into areas where larger differences can be found. Because overall there was so little difference between the stations, one station was arbitrarily chosen for the test.

One final step of planning proved to be necessary. The team had available 240 cans with stringers, or 10 cans for each of the 24 heads. Team members believed they could tell a good can from a bad one. But was that the way the process would see it? In other words, could the team be assured that so-called good cans would actually be defect free? These questions prompted the team to decide to collect 960 good cans, a relatively easy step because so few cans had oxide stringers in the rim area. Thus, the team had available 40 "good" cans and 10 cans with stringers for each of the 24 filling/sealing heads.

This type of careful planning is a mark of good problem solvers. The planning and preparation for the experiment took more than a month. Collecting and marking samples, modifying the equipment to indicate which head filled and sealed which can and obtaining permission from company management all required considerable time and effort. Such planning ensures that when a problem-solving team completes an experiment, it has confidence in the results. Industrial experiments also require careful coordination with company management. Production facilities are put in place to produce salable product, not to run experiments. Thus, another characteristic of competent industrial problem solvers is that they respect production management's responsibilities and are willing to spend time to assure that running the experiment is practical and does not unnecessarily disturb production requirements.

[†]Station-to-station variation was determined by comparing the percentage of cans from each station that exceeded the maximum leakage rate specification.

Running the Experiment

The team could have decided to run the "good" cans first followed by the "bad" ones, the worst possible decision. Reversing this order has no more merit. Running an experiment in clusters of good followed by bad or the reverse supposes that the process will stay absolutely constant during the course of the experiment—probably an erroneous assumption. Some members of the team were willing to follow a simple rotation scheme of four "good" cans and one "bad" can. As it turned out, this method would have worked. But there is always the possibility that any cyclical scheme will coincide with cyclical variations in the process. Considering all the work that had gone into the experiment, it would have been unwise to take this risk when a risk-free method was readily at hand. The best approach, in cases such as this, is to mix the bad product and good product together randomly. By random mixing, the results cannot erroneously be confounded or mixed up with cyclical patterns in the process itself.

During the experiment, none of the 960 "good" cans proved to be leakers[§] while 93 of the 240 cans with stringers leaked. Some filling/sealing heads (numbers 1 and 4) were fed 10 cans with stringers and produced no leakers. Head number 24 had 10 out of 10 leakers. The others had defect rates between zero and 10. The cause of the leaking cans was determined to be an interaction between two key variables—filling/sealing heads that were marginally adjusted and cans that had stringers at the rim.

Whenever a can was found to be a leaker, the leak always occurred at the point of the oxide stringer. Investigation also determined that filling/sealing heads which had zero leakers out of 10 cans with stringers and those heads which produced 10 leakers out of 10 cans with stringers had filled and sealed cans with all three grades of stringers. The size of the stringer was not a factor in whether a can leaked. In retrospect, the team realized that it did not need to measure and identify the size of the stringer, only note its presence. If the size of the stringer had been important, however, but had not been recorded, a major portion of the clues to the problem would have been lost and there would have been no practical way to reconstruct the results. It is always better to get somewhat more detail at the beginning of an investigation than too little.

[§]As noted earlier in this chapter, the word "leak" (or "leaker") means that the escape of carbon dioxide from the can exceeded allowable rates. There was no leakage of beer.

Correcting the Problem

The team next performed a thorough investigation comparing various dimensions, spring tensions, etc., between the filling/sealing heads that produced no leakers out of 10 cans with oxide stringers and those heads that produced 10 leakers out of 10 cans with oxide stringers.

Initially, the team had reason to believe that if there were no stringers in the rim area a tight seal would be made when the lid was applied, even though they knew that no two of the 24 heads were exactly alike in spring tension, flatness, squareness, edge smoothness, geometry and the like. However, once these measurements were taken, the team determined the correct specifications from those heads that could make non-leaking cans even with aluminum that contained oxide stringers in the critical rim area.

One essential step remained—a quality audit under production conditions. After the filling/sealing heads were adjusted to the specifications derived from the best performers, the team observed an entire day's production of several million cans. The result: not a single leaking can. In the past there would have been as many as 200. A second day's test with no reported leaks confirmed that the team had indeed discovered the key variables and had derived the correct specifications.

Summary

It is important to emphasize that the correct specifications came from the process itself—not from the engineers. This approach is based on "consulting with the process" to determine those conditions that will always produce good product. However, while this experiment was technically interesting and even innovative, an important lesson was that management determines the quality level. The management of the company had considered any defective product unacceptable. The problem-solving team, knowing management's position, solved a seemingly impossible problem at a cost that was small compared to the potential deterioration of the company's quality reputation.

CHAPTER 7

Designed Experiments

It is not unusual for a large number of process variables to be eliminated as possible key variables during multi-vari analysis. But even if only two or three process variables remain under consideration, determining which of them—or their interactions—are the cause of process problems can present real difficulties. In these cases, multi-vari followed by a designed (or factorial) experiment usually provides the most direct solution.

Figure 9 shows a balanced designed experiment with four variables each at two levels. In this figure there are 16 (2^4) test combinations to be run.

		A-		A+	
		B-	B+	B-	B+
C-	D-				
	D+				
C+	D-				
	D+				

Figure 9. Designed Experiment Layout Grid. In this figure, A, B, C and D represent process variables such as temperature, pressure, time, etc. A+, B−, etc., represent the high or low test limits for the variable. The open squares represent numbers that reflect the results of a particular test: for example, the upper left-hand box represents the results of testing at conditions A−, B−, C− and D−.

Conventional Testing	Designed Experiment
1. A	1. A
2. B	2. B
3. C	3. C
4. D	4. D
	5. A X B
	6. A X C
	7. A X D
	8. B X C
	9. B X D
	10. C X D
	11. A X B X C
	12. A X B X D
	13. B X C X D
	14. A X C X D
	15. A X B X C X D
	16. RESIDUAL ERROR

Figure 10. Comparison of the Amount of Test Information Provided by Conventional Testing and by a Designed Experiment

Figure 10 compares the results of conventional testing with statistically designed experiments.* In conventional testing, investigators attempt to gain information about variables A, B, C, and D, one at a time. A statistically designed experiment, such as that shown in Figure 9, provides information about A, B, C, D and also determines if there are any two-factor and three-factor interactions. If a second replicate is run, then the four-factor effects free of residual error can be estimated.

The concept of "residual error" is another important element in understanding designed experiments. The amount of residual error in a designed experiment indicates whether the test design included the correct variable(s). If there is a high residual error—that is, a lot of "noise" in the experiment—the results are saying that something else besides the variables being evaluated is causing the excessive

*For a thorough discussion of designed experiments, see Anderson, Virgil and McLean, Robert A., *Design of Experiments* (New York:Marcel Dekker, Inc., 1974, with the American Society for Quality Control, Milwaukee, WI).

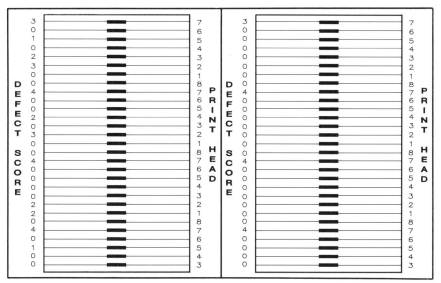

Figure 11. Component Printing Defect Scores Before Cleaning

Figure 12. Component Printing Defect Scores After Cleaning

variation. Therefore, the experiment itself tells the investigators how well it was designed and run. This is important because designed experiments can be run with the wrong variables—usually the result of "guessing" at the cause of the problem. While these guesses can be helpful in eliminating some variables, the purpose of a designed experiment is to see how much the variables being tested contribute to the variation or if untested variables contribute greatly. In other words, in a designed experiment, the investigator can determine whether the "signal"—the selected variable(s)—stands out above the "noise"—the variables not tested.

The concept of separating the effect of the variables being tested from the residual error can be difficult to understand. Many people have trouble understanding how investigators can analyze test results to tell which variables and/or interactions are real (significant) and which ones have little or no effect on the results.

The following example illustrates how real effects can be separated from residual error or "noise." A company was using an eight-station printer to print identifying information on electronic components. In Figure 11 a group of 29 components is shown in the rectangle at the center of the figure. The numbers to the right of the rectangle indicate the print head (1-8) on which each component was printed. The degree of printing defectiveness is shown by the numbers to the left of the rectangle; the defect score runs from 0 (no defect) to 4 (maximum defect). Of the 29 components, 12 show some degree of printing defect. This was considered an unacceptable defect rate. In an attempt to eliminate the defects, the company called in an industrial investigator to evaluate the process. As a part of the evaluation, the investigator suggested ultrasonically cleaning the 29 components in Freon. Figure 12 shows the components after the cleaning. The cleaning had physically removed the residual error—that is, eight of the small printing defects—so that the real culprit, head number 7, stands out as the source of the problem. In Figure 11, the real effect, at head number 7, was partially masked by small defects caused by the "noise" from other heads. When company personnel had looked at Figure 11 they did not realize that they were seeing a combination of real effect and residual error.

In the same way, the analysis of a designed experiment separates—mathematically—the significant variables from random noise and places confidence limits on the results of the experiment. Designed experiments are used, in part, to accomplish mathematically what in the electronic component printing example was accomplished physically.

CHAPTER 8

The Case of Porous Decorative Rings

A company was experiencing an increased level of porosity in the cast decorative rings which it manufactured. Production requirements had increased, and the company was having trouble meeting the demand because scrap rates were too high. A high scrap rate had always existed, but it had not been considered serious because defective rings were returned to the molten metal and remelted. However, with the increased production requirements the company could not afford the extra time to recast many rings. The foreman who had supervised the area for many years and had recently retired had been brought back as a consultant. To find the solution to the problem he experimented with process variables such as pouring rate, pouring height and the temperature of the molten metal. One of the two suppliers of metal had been notified that the composition of raw material had apparently changed. The consultant foreman had tried every modification he knew and was concerned that he would have to resort to the "old timers" remedy: when all else fails, throw a potato into the molten metal. To help resolve the problem, company management brought in a problem-solving team. When the team arrived in the casting area, the inspectors were rejecting most of the rings for excess porosity and these rings were being remelted.

Quantification

The team determined that the first step in its problem-solving strategy should be quantification. The team collected samples of rings which showed varying degrees of porosity and developed the following numerical rating scale:

    1 — Very Small Defect
    2 — Obvious Defect
    3 — Large Defect
    4 — Very Large Defect
    5 — Huge Hole

It was decided that each defect would be rated and a tally kept of the defect scores. In addition, the location of the defect would be plotted in red on a picture of the ring. This type of diagram is known as a measles chart.

After developing the rating scale and pictorial representation, the team conducted a multi-vari study. During the study, the team gathered samples of rings in order to determine patterns of variation. The following types of variation were examined: within-ring, ring-to-ring and time-to-time. It is extremely important to look at within-piece (within-ring) variation, whenever possible. In this case, it was necessary to identify the location and size of individual defects. Too often, insufficient information is gathered on within-piece variation and important clues are lost.

Test Results

Figure 13 shows the measles chart. The numbers within the ring are the average total defect scores for the entire multi-vari study. These numbers were derived by multiplying the occurrence of a defect on each ring by its defect score. For example, a ring might have one defect with a score of 5, one defect with a score of 4 and one defect with a score of 3. The defect score for this ring would therefore be 12. Six occurrences of defects each with a score of 2 would also result in a score of 12. An average is shown because the team found there was so little variation from ring to ring and time to time that an average was representative. The largest variation was within ring.

For the entire study the average defect score per ring was 19.6, and the numbers shown within the ring in Figure 13 reflect average defect scores for each area. For example, the number 12.9 reflects the average defect score for the top half of the ring: i.e., the part of the ring above the horizontal line. The number 6.7 reflects the average defect score for the bottom half of the ring: i.e., below the horizontal line. The sum of the top half and bottom half scores (12.9 + 6.7) = 19.6. The number 6.1 reflects the average score for the right-hand half of the ring: i.e., the part of the ring to the right of the vertical line. Scores for the right- and left-hand halves of the ring

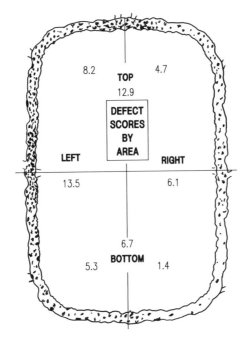

Figure 13. Measles Chart for Ring Defects

(13.5 + 6.1) also total 19.6. In the same way, each of the four quadrants are scored: e.g., the upper right-hand quadrant has a score of 4.7. The total average score for the four quadrants (8.2 + 4.7 + 5.3 + 1.4) also totals 19.6.

The left side of the ring has about twice the average total defect score that the right side has (13.5 versus 6.1) and the top of the ring has about twice the defect score that the bottom of the ring has (12.9 versus 6.7).

If the upper left-hand quadrant of the ring is compared to the lower right-hand quadrant the ratio is about 6 to 1 (8.2 versus 1.4). The other two opposite quadrants are approximately equal, 5.3 versus 4.7. A closer look at the spots on the measles chart shows that the greatest concentration of defects (porosity) occurred around the upper left-hand corner.

When the pattern of defects was quite clear, a team member pointed out that there seemed to be something unusual about the upper left-hand corner of the casting and asked if anyone had any ideas. The foreman said, "Yes, that is where the fan is." When questioned about the fan, the foreman reminded the team that working over molten metal is very hot work, and a fan must be used to cool off the operator. Also, with a fan in place the rings can be taken out of the mold sooner because they solidify more quickly. The team also asked if the operator ever used more than one fan or no fan at all. The foreman stated that operators could not work without fans for very long, and in the summer another fan directly in front of the operator was often used.

The Designed Experiment

In many cases the multi-vari study itself does not solve the problem, but it rules out variables that do not fit and suggests the type of variables that do fit the clues. In this case, the fact that the defects were concentrated in one area reduced the likelihood that the problem was caused by variables such as the supplier of the raw material. The pattern of variation on the measles chart strongly suggested that something was different in the upper left area, and the fan was the most likely suspect. The team then designed an experiment to investigate the effect of the fan on the porosity. The team decided to conduct the experiment in groups of five rings in a row under four different conditions:
1. With the fan in its typical location, near the upper left area of the mold
2. With no fan
3. With the front fan only
4. With both fans.

The next step was to use a random number table to select the numbers 1, 2, 3 and 4 to determine the order of using the fans. The foreman explained the test to the operator and assured him that the team would ask him to operate with no fan for only groups of five rings at a time on three occasions. The team chose to run the 20 rings (five in a row at four conditions) three times in order to obtain a different random order each time for the four conditions. By running the experiment three times the team hoped it would be able to "turn the problem on and off."

Figure 14 shows the results of the designed experiment in the form of a multi-vari chart. From 8:30 a.m. to 9:30 a.m. the team ran five rings in a row with the left (regular) fan in place, then ran five in a row with no fans, then five in a row with both fans and finished with five in a row with the front fan only. The team reran the test in a different random order from 10:45 to 11:45 a.m. During both sets of tests, when only the front fan ran, the defects were significantly less than under the other three conditions. The results of the second test

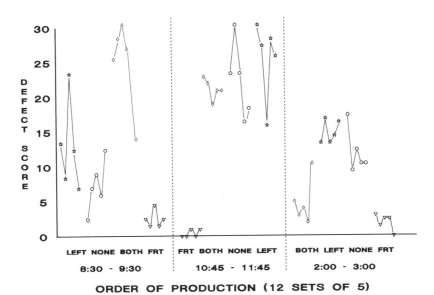

Figure 14. Decorative Ring Defect Study

run were more dramatic than those of the first run. From 2:00 to 3:00 p.m. the team ran a third test and again found that the best results occurred when only the front fan was running. The team had let the process do the talking and had listened to it. The process clearly told the team that when only the front fan was used, the defects were drastically reduced. When investigators do not listen to the process they sometimes miss the real causes of problems and use myths to explain them. The idea of throwing a potato into the molten metal is an example of one of these myths.

From production management's perspective, the problem-solving strategy was successful. By using only the front fan the new porosity defect rate was so low that production requirements could easily be met. In fact, the defect rate was so low that essentially all the rings were acceptable. However, 100 percent inspection was still used to find the few remaining defective rings. In addition to being costly, 100 percent inspection is not completely effective. It is likely that if production management had the team conduct further investigations they might have eliminated the porosity or at least reduced it to such an insignificant level that 100 percent inspection could have been eliminated. The team could have experimented with the front fan by moving it to different heights, angles, distances, speeds, etc., as well as trying various size fans.

When the team first looked at the operation it was told that rejections were higher than usual. However, because records were not normally kept it was possible that rejections had not increased but due to higher production requirements the rejections were noticed more. Since the company previously did not have a well-defined numerical scale for determining the degree of porosity, it is also possible that the higher rejection rate simply reflected the increased inspection attention. It is also likely that before the study the difference between accepted and rejected rings was minimal and all rings had too much porosity.

CHAPTER 9

The Case of Scrapped Artillery Projectiles

A company that manufactured artillery projectiles was concerned about the potential harm that poor quality could cause and thus called in an industrial investigator to help improve the quality of its product. The company's primary concern lay with the variation in wall thickness which determined how accurately the projectiles would fly.

The manufacturing process started with five-inch-diameter bars of cold rolled steel sawed to a length that weighed about 26 pounds. This "slug" was put into a machine and formed cold. All units went onto a common conveyor and were then measured by mounting them in a fixture with a dial indicator against the outside wall and a fixed stop against the inside wall. By rotating the projectile, the dial indicator continuously read the wall thickness. The maximum difference allowed between the thickest and thinnest part of the wall was 0.044 in. The month before the investigator arrived, 10,000 projectiles from the five cold forming machines had been scrapped because they exceeded the variation limit.

The technical person responsible for the operation stated that the five cold forming machines were old and temperamental. He suggested that they had personalities of their own, and no one knew what they were going to do next. After discussing the problem with him, the investigator suggested running a multi-vari study. The study began by taking five cold-formed slugs in a row at 9:00 a.m. and 1:00 p.m. (the first shift) and at 4:00 p.m. (the second shift) from each of the five machines. Figure 15 shows the results from three of the five machines: the best machine, the worst machine and the middle machine. The piece-to-piece variation is connected by solid lines and the time-to-time variation is indicated by dashed lines.

As Figure 15 indicates, there was very little time-to-time and shift-to-shift variation. In fact, with all the piece-to-piece variation it is surprising that the time-to-time results were as consistent as they were. Because machine-to-machine variation was significant, a best and worst machine could be designated. Time-to-time and shift-to-shift variation, however, were not significant. The piece-to-piece variation on the best machine was relatively small compared to the

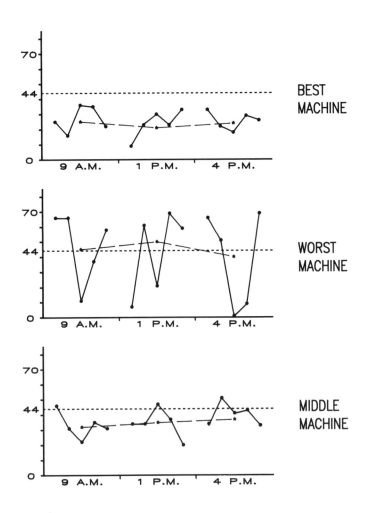

Figure 15. Multi-Vari Chart of Projectile Wall Thickness Variations

large piece-to-piece variation on the worst machine. Thus, piece-to-piece variation depended on the machine. When the word "depends" is required to describe an effect, an interaction is present. Interactions cause many of the unsolved problems in industry.

Two clues to the problem were now apparent: there was a difference in the machines, and something was interacting with these machines. Interestingly, four of the lowest readings came from the worst machine. At this point the investigator asked, "What could be interacting with the machines?" One possible interaction with the machine was the out-of-squareness of the sawed face of the slugs in relation to the edge of the bars from which they were sawed. A saw, unlike a milling machine, can act like a serrated knife cutting a watermelon and can cause considerable out-of-squareness.

The Designed Experiment

The investigator used the two clues provided by the multi-vari study to design an experiment of two variables at each of two levels. The two variables selected for the designed experiment were the out-of-squareness of the sawed slugs and the condition of the machines. The two levels of out-of-squareness were the squarest slugs that could be found and the most out-of-square slugs. The two levels of machine condition were the best and worst machines. The squarest and most out-of-square slugs and only the best and worst machines were used because knowledge often lies in the extremes. In this case, the investigator would not have learned more by studying intermediate levels of out-of-squareness nor the three machines between the best and worst.

The conditions of the designed experiment were run in a random order to prevent some unknown factor from invalidating the test. When the square slugs were run on the best machine the result was a low amount of wall thickness variation averaging about 0.005 in. and also very consistent results from one slug to the next (see Figure 16). When the square slugs were run on the worst machine, the results were again consistent, though at a much higher level—about 0.037 in. From this data, it was apparent to the investigator that the plungers on the cold forming machines were misaligned. When the out-of-square slugs were run, variation increased. However, since all square slugs in the worst machine resulted in an average of 0.037 in. variation in wall thickness, the machine must have been, in effect, misaligned 0.037 in. Similarly, the best machine must have been, in effect, misaligned about 0.005 in.

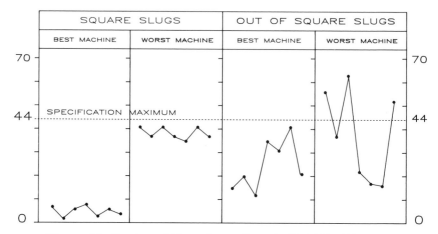

Figure 16. Designed Experiment Data in Multi-Vari Format

The investigator reasoned that as the plunger of the cold forming machine hit the face of a slug it could either accent the out-of-squareness or compensate for it, depending on the angle at which the plunger hit the face. This would explain why some results from the worst machine could be very good. The misaligned plunger on the machine and the out-of-squareness of the slugs were either cancelling or adding to each other. The results confirmed the theory that out-of-square slugs were interacting with the misalignment of the machine. However, there was an interaction beyond the amount of out-of-squareness that related to how the out-of-squareness was oriented to the misalignment.

To confirm this interaction—slug orientation with machine misalignment—the investigator obtained slugs and measured their out-of-squareness and marked which way they were out of square. The investigator then put the slugs into the worst machine in a way that the misalignment and out-of-squareness would add to one another. Next, out-of-square slugs were placed in the worst machine so that the misalignment and out-of-squareness would tend toward cancelling each other. Therefore, the results depended on how the misalignment of the machine was oriented to the out-of-squareness of the slug.

Review of Designed Experiments

All properly conducted designed experiments contain four key elements:

1. For practical analysis they must be balanced.

2. To be valid they must be randomized.

3. To give a good estimate of repeatability, more than one replication (more than one test at each set of conditions) should be conducted.

4. A numerical system for measuring attributes and/or dimensions is required. The use of satisfactory or unsatisfactory attribute notation is not sensitive enough and is a major reason that many industrial problems remain unsolved. An agreed-upon numerical system for measuring attributes is necessary. Dimensional measurements usually have agreed-upon numerical systems such as ohms, inches or pounds, but in some situations numerical systems must be developed.

To apply these four elements to the designed experiment just described:

1. The experiment was balanced because the same number of projectiles (seven) was used in each of the four combinations.

2. A random number table was used to decide the order in which the test conditions would be run. If the order in which the test conditions were run had not been randomized, some other variable might have changed during the test, and the investigator would not have known it. In Figure 16, the results generally became worse moving from "left to right." Without randomization the investigator might have suspected that things were getting worse as time went on. By randomly returning to the four conditions, and the results coming back to where they were the last time that condition was tested, the test indicated that the test condition—not some other uncontrolled variable—caused the variation.

3. Seven replicates were tested. Whenever there is a large amount of variation, it is best to test many replicates. The large variation in Figure 15 indicated that a number of replicates was required. This was important because some of the best (lowest) readings on the out-of-square slugs on the worst machine were lower than the worst (highest) readings with the out-of-square slugs on the best machine. If only three replicates had been run and only the lowest three readings of the out-of-square slugs on the worst machine and only the highest three readings of the out-of-square slugs on the best machine had been obtained, the investigator might have erroneously concluded that with out-of-square slugs it was better to use the worst machine. This error would have rendered the test results worse than useless— they would have been misleading.

4. The study already included a system for measuring the thickness of the wall all around the circumference of the projectile. If there had

not been a system for measuring this dimension, the investigator would have had to devise one.

Turning the Problem on and off

Before a manufacturing problem can be considered solved, it must be able to be "turned on and off." In this case, then, the next step was for the investigator to demonstrate that he could turn the problem on and off. The investigator used the worst machine and asked the technical person how he wanted the next projectile to turn out. He said he wanted a very good one. Since the investigator now knew the machine's misalignment, and in which direction it was misaligned, he chose a slug that had a large amount of out-of-squareness and lined it up so that the out-of-squareness of the slug and the misalignment of the machine would tend toward cancelling each other. The result was quite good. The technical person thought that the investigator was lucky and asked him to make another projectile—this time a bad one. A slug very much out-of-square was rotated to the opposite direction so that the out-of-squareness and misalignment added to each other. This time the resulting projectile was quite bad. The investigator proceeded in this way until it was agreed that he could predict how a projectile would turn out.

The investigator then used square slugs in each machine to determine the amount and direction of misalignment. The machines were adjusted using square slugs as test samples. The investigator also placed a median chart on the cold forming machines and on the saw line so squareness could be controlled. The month following these adjustments the number of rejects was 18, compared to 10,000 rejects on a similar production volume at the start of the study.

Summary

From the results of the multi-vari study and designed experiment it was clear that the problem had two components: the machines were misaligned and the non-square slugs were interacting with the misaligned machines. The interaction effect was a mystery to the people operating the machines because sometimes a machine yielded a bad result and sometimes a good result. Because the slugs were out-of-square a widely varying amount no one knew how much the machines were misaligned. The investigator was able to use square slugs to determine the amount and direction of misalignment and correct each machine. Even if the slugs were out-of-square a small amount, good results could still be obtained.

It had been common practice for the operators to get onto the machines and use a sledgehammer to drive shims in to align the machine. However, with unknown amounts of out-of-squareness and the random orientation of the face of the slug, no one knew exactly how much a machine was misaligned nor in which direction. The investigator did not change the method of shimming the machines, but now the operators knew how much to shim and in what direction. The use of square slugs ensured that the proper shims were in place.

As previously mentioned, a manufacturing problem cannot be considered solved until it can be turned on and off. Too frequently in industry when a major problem exists people change a dozen things and the defect level goes down. Then they cross their fingers, walk away and hope the problem does not return. There are two reasons that people walk away from the problem. First, they do not really know which of the dozen things helped, and they do not want anyone changing anything because the problem might reappear. However, most problems do return because they were not solved—they were temporarily "beaten into submission." A second reason people walk away is because management assigns them to a "hotter fire," rather than allowing them the time to find the real cause, and, ultimately, a solution to prevent the return of the problem. Management usually reasons that "the fire is out, so why waste time on it?" Unfortunately, this common practice allows the fire to return again and again.

CHAPTER 10

The Case of Shorts on Dust Cover Seals

In the following case, quantification of defects helped solve the problem that one company had with a high scrap rate on injection-molded dust cover seals. The operations personnel of the company were convinced that raw material composition was the cause of the problem because there had been a recent change in suppliers.

The investigator who had been called in suggested running a multi-vari study to determine the type of variation, such as within-piece; within-mold (from one cavity to the next); shot-to-shot; heat-to-heat; time-to-time throughout the day; or from one batch of raw material to another. Operations personnel suspected the raw material because they felt they had previously achieved better results.

A number of problems were encountered during the plastic molding operation. These problems included such visual defects as shorts, distortion, blisters, splits and thick flash. Thick flash was not actually a defect, but it wastes material and therefore is undesirable. The initial diagnostic step was to establish a numerical scale to rate these defects. If the product had no defects, it was rated a 0; a minor defect (but not rejectable) was a 1; a barely rejectable defect was a 2; a major defect was a 3; and a severe defect was a 4.

The investigator decided to record and plot the defect score for "shorts" because it was the largest defect category on the Pareto chart (see Figure 17). A data sheet showing the position of the 16 cavities in the mold was drawn so that defect location and severity could be plotted in a technique similar to a measles chart. Figure 18 presents that data sheet showing results at 10:17 a.m. At that time, the only defects were on the "right-hand" side of the seals, suggesting the occurrence of within-piece variation. In addition, of the 16 cavities, the two defective seals were on the right-hand side of the mold in the center, suggesting there was also within-mold variation.

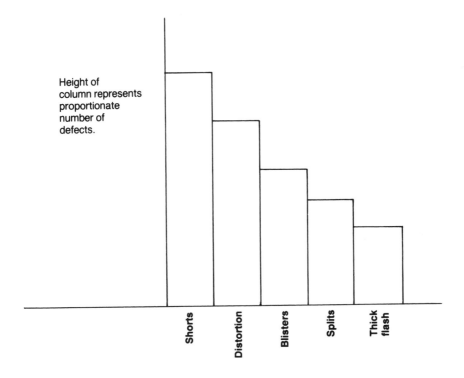

Height of column represents proportionate number of defects.

Shorts | Distortion | Blisters | Splits | Thick flash

Figure 17. Pareto Chart of Molding Defects

Figure 19 shows a heat which was run at 4:06 p.m. and indicates that the area containing defects had spread out. This pattern pointed to a possible problem with the way the two halves of the mold fit together, a temperature problem which existed to a different extent at different times (that is, time-to-time variation) or perhaps an interaction between the two variables.

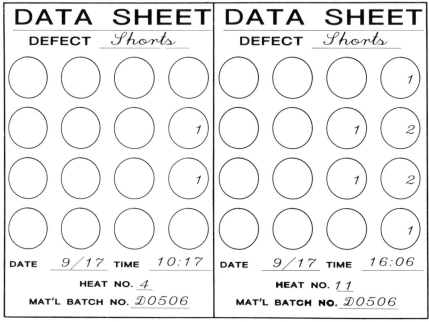

Figure 18. Defect Chart
Data Sheet for 10:17 a.m.

Figure 19. Defect Chart
Data Sheet for 4:06 p.m.

Using the Clues

The investigator now had several clues: the severity of the problem seemed to vary from time to time, though time-to-time variation might actually be heat-to-heat variation since each time was a different heat. The cause of the problem had something to do with location and position because the location of the defect was positional within the cavity and positional within the mold. All of these clues, plus the fact that the same raw material was used for both runs (heats), pointed out that the process variable originally suspected—a change in raw material—was not the cause of the problem. The investigator determined that there were two key variables—excessive variation in the temperature of the injected plastic and an improper fit of the mold halves.

Summary

This case demonstrates an important difference between the traditional engineering approach to problem solving and the key variable isolation approach. The traditional approach looks for the causes of product problems by running one day on one raw material, machine setting or condition, and then running another raw material, machine setting or condition the next day. But too often with the traditional approach, many factors change between the two runs. With the key variable isolation approach, first a numerical rating scale for visual and physical attributes is developed. Then investigators evaluate the product in much more detail, use a much smaller sample size and run for a specific, short period of time without changing process conditions. If evaluation of variation over a longer term is required, another small sample can be taken later. The key variable isolation approach provides numerical data which is used to eliminate unimportant variables and focus on the specific variables—the key variable(s)—that are causing the defects in the product.

CHAPTER 11

The Case of Rejects on a Multicavity Compression Molder

A manufacturer of molded plastic components used several multicavity forming machines for molding tamperproof covers for containers. After they were formed, the covers were dropped into a bucket. A random sample then was taken from the bucket for visual and dimensional inspection. Despite this inspection, some of the company's customers had complained about visual and/or dimensional defects. Because of these complaints, the company assembled a problem-solving team.

The Multi-Vari Study

In its investigation the team viewed each cavity as if it were a separate process. This was an important decision because any cavity might produce units different from another cavity. Before the team was assembled, production personnel had believed that the inspection procedure included the drawing of a random sample from a single process. In fact, relatively few samples were drawn from numerous separate lots or processes.

As is usual with an ongoing process, the team chose to run a multi-vari study to investigate patterns of variation in the covers. The multi-vari study looked at within-piece variation, cavity-to-cavity variation, cycle-to-cycle variation, short-term time-to-time variation, longer term time-to-time variation and machine-to-machine variation. In this case, the team found that there were two significant problems: excessive dimensional variation and visual defects. By their very nature, the physical dimensions were already on a numerical scale. However, evaluating the visual defects required the creation of a numerical scale for rating each defect. The team took additional time to prepare this numerical scale before beginning the multi-vari study. Visual defects evaluated included plastic "strings," feathering, flash, bent edges, edges damaged from stripping and holes (short shots).

The results of the multi-vari study on the visual defects showed mostly time-to-time variation, while the important dimensional characteristics indicated mostly cavity-to-cavity variation. These results clearly separated the corrective action into two categories: corrective action for visual defects, and corrective action for excessive dimensional variation. The visual defects variation (time-to-time) related to process variables such as temperature, time and pressure. The dimensional variation primarily involved the construction of the individual cavity. The size of each cavity determined what dimensions would be made in that cavity. Differences in dimensional characteristics were built into the cavities. Therefore, adjusting process variables such as mold temperature or injection pressure did not significantly affect the dimensions.

Reducing Dimensional Variation

If a cavity was damaged and then replaced, there was a new "machine" (actually, a new process) producing parts with different dimensions. The cavities could not all be made exactly the same but the team found that the cavity-to-cavity dimensional variation was more than expected and more than should be allowed. The corrective action for the excessive dimensional variation focused on reworking or replacing problem cavities.

Correcting Visual Defects

To determine the proper process variable settings for eliminating visual defects, the team designed and ran an experiment called a "process latitude" or tolerance analysis study. The purpose of the latitude study was to determine if the process specifications for temperature, pressure, etc., were correct. The process variables in the experiment were forming pressure, holding pressure, temperature profile, pin cooling temperature and cavity cooling temperature. All five process variables were run at two levels, low and high. The team set the low and high test levels at the limits of the accepted process variables (e.g., lowest permitted cavity temperature and highest permitted cavity temperature) to determine what effect the full range of these variables had on the various visual characteristics. The specification limits of the variables were used because these were the process variation ranges that normally occurred.

In a designed experiment with five variables each at two levels, there are 32 (i.e., 2^5) test conditions. Sixteen of the 32 conditions were run and from this study the team was able to determine what the specifications should be. This is a fractional factorial designed experiment—½ of 2^5. A classic fractional factorial experiment was appropriate to use because the team was interested in these five variables only and was certain the key variables were included in those five.

Of the five variables, one was found to have a moderate effect and one had a drastic effect on the visual defects. The variable that produced a drastic effect had specification limits that were too wide, so the team narrowed the specification and retested to determine more realistic limits. In contrast, the team found that the remaining three variables had little or no effect on the visual defects even though the process limits were tested. The team was able to substantially widen the specification limits for the three variables after retesting. These new, wider specification limits simplified processing, thereby saving time and money without having a negative effect on the visual characteristics.

The key variables in this case study are intentionally not identified. In other situations the effects or interactions of other process variables such as make or type of molding machine, amount and type of additives or fillers in the raw plastic (e.g., stearates, glass fiber, etc.), percentage of reground plastic, mold design and so forth will be different from those in this case study. What is important is that two process variables caused the overwhelming majority of the visual defects in this case study and those two variables were identified by the problem-solving team so that appropriate corrective action could be taken.

Summary

In this case, the manufacturer's problem involved complaints of excessive dimensional variation and visual defects in the product. To resolve the problem, the team:

- Determined that the sampling procedure previously used did not fit the actual process conditions
- Developed a system so that visual defects could be rated numerically
- Ran a multi-vari study to determine the patterns of both dimensional and visual defects variation

- Ran a fractional designed experiment to pinpoint the causes of the visual defects.

The results of the multi-vari and designed experiment studies showed that:

- Attempts to force corrections in dimensions by changing process variables such as temperature or pressure were not successful and might only make the problem of visual defects worse.
- Certain cavities had to be reworked or replaced to reduce the amount of overall dimensional variation to acceptable limits.
- One process variable had to be respecified to narrower limits to eliminate the problem of visual defects, but three variables were set to wider limits to make processing easier.

CHAPTER 12

The Case of Varying Seat Measurements

The following case involved excessive variation in an important characteristic called a seat dimension of a forged part. The seat dimension is formed in a forging press and is crucial for further processing. In this case, inconsistent seat dimensions had led to processing problems, and an in-house team comprised of the engineer, quality controller and production foreman had been assigned the job of solving the problem.

The manufacturing operation started with the operator placing 30 parts in a tray and then setting the tray on a rotating table in an oven. The parts came out of the oven extremely hot and sat near the opening of the oven. While air was drawn into the oven over the parts the operator used tongs to pick them up, one at a time, and place them into the forging press. The operator then forged each one, dropped it into a container and returned for another. By the time the operator picked up the last parts, they had cooled quite a bit with the air drawn past them into the oven accelerating the cooling process.

The engineer maintained that the seat dimension variation was caused by excessive cooling. He felt that it was necessary to devise a method to keep the parts constantly hot to avoid the problem. He had begun work on a constant temperature device that would involve design, procurement and installation time as well as incur expenses. However, the engineer believed that this device would solve only part of the problem.

The engineer felt that the operator caused much of the problem by placing the parts in the forging press inconsistently. Because the operator worked piecework, he or she ran them in and out of the forging press quickly and did not take the time to position each one carefully. Therefore, the engineer had also begun designing a device that would hold the part in the forging press at the "correct" distance. The estimated cost of this device was $30,000 and it would have taken about six months to build. The engineer felt this second device would solve the rest of the problem. His strategy, unfortunately, was a typical example of blaming the operator and then designing out operator influence.

In order to expedite problem-solving efforts, an outside investigator was called in to assist the in-house team. The investigator began by asking the engineer how the seat dimension of each part was measured and learning that a vernier caliper was used to measure across the middle of the seat. The investigator explained that when a vernier caliper is used a burr or flash from the forging operation can result in an inaccurate measurement. He suggested that a pointed micrometer would be more accurate because a burr or flash would not be measured. The engineer agreed, so the measurement system was changed.

The Multi-Vari Study

Once the measurement system was in place, the investigator suggested running a multi-vari study. The engineer and investigator agreed to measure each seat in three places—the top, the middle and the bottom of the forged area—to study within-piece (within-part) variation. To study part-to-part variation, the investigator chose to measure five parts in a row. It was also decided that the first and the last five parts would be taken out of a tray in order to study any effect of temperature. The study was scheduled to be run throughout the day and on second shift to determine time-to-time and shift-to-shift variation. Before the study began, the engineer stated, "I really don't like to run tests when I already know the answer." The investigator assured him that if the data proved consistent with the engineer's own hypothesis, he could use these results to convince others of his case.

The operator and quality controller started the multi-vari study by measuring the first five parts in a row in the tray and the last five in a row in the tray. The results from 10:30 a.m. are shown in Figure 20. An O is used for readings at the top of the seat, an X for readings in the middle and a ■ for readings at the bottom of the seat. By the time the first five readings were plotted, the investigator asked the engineer if he realized that the die was faulty. The investigator stated, "You're supposed to be making a parallel unit. The top and middle

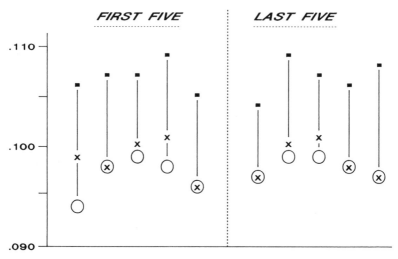

Figure 20. Seat Dimension Multi-Vari Study — Comparison of First Five Parts to Last Five Parts

dimensions are very close to being the same, but the bottom dimension is much larger due to the shape of the die." The engineer replied, "Yes, the way they hand grind them that could easily happen." After the last five readings from the first tray were plotted, the investigator noted that, "the first five and the last five have very little difference between them. It doesn't seem that sitting and cooling in the tray makes much, if any, difference."

Figure 21 shows the time-to-time variation. The dimensions of the five piece samples were averaged so the time-to-time variation throughout the day could be more easily detected. Measurements are also made during the second shift, which started at 3:30 p.m., so shift-to-shift variation could be seen as well. When the measurements of the first five parts are compared to the last five from a given tray, it is quite clear that temperature, within the range that was being tested, made no significant difference. The main difference lay in the shape of the die. Some time-to-time variation occurred, but it was small in comparison to the within-piece variation. The engineer was reluctant to accept the fact that the temperature did not make any difference and noted that the effect of placement in the forging press had not been tested. "Possibly the operator, who had the quality controller watching him, placed all the parts in the forging press about the right distance. We are obtaining this $30,000 device to ensure that the operator will always put them in properly," the engineer commented.

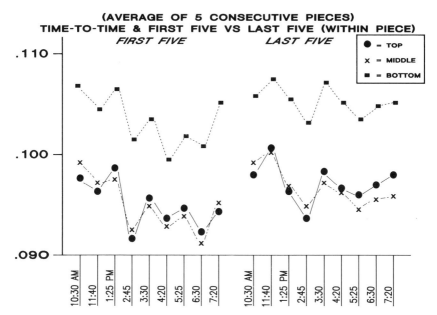

Figure 21. Seat Dimension Multi-Vari Study — Time-to-Time Variation

The Designed Experiment

The investigator and engineer then decided to design an experiment to test the effect of the varying distances of the parts within the forging press because the multi-vari study had ruled out temperature as a key variable and demonstrated that the greatest variation was within piece. A designed experiment was used because the investigator and engineer had to intentionally change the distances the operator placed the units in the forging press. Each tray contained 30 parts so it was agreed that 10 would be placed in the forging press at the right distance, 10 "in too far" and 10 "not in far enough." The order of running the designed experiment was selected by using a random number table.

The results of the designed experiment are shown in Figure 22. The top and middle of all seat dimensions averaged 0.098 in. Whether the parts were in too far, at the correct distance or out too far, essentially there was no difference in the results of the designed experiment. It is rare for industrial data to be so consistent. The major variation was within the part, the same result as had been obtained earlier. The

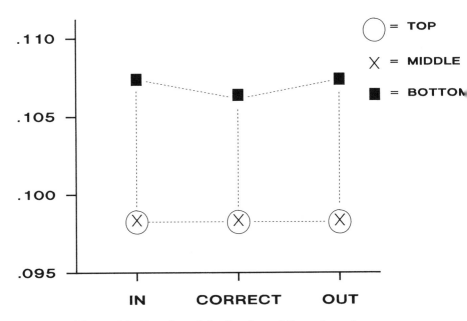

Figure 22. Results of the Designed Experiment

engineer asked the quality controller if he had made sure the operator put the parts both in too far and not in far enough. The quality controller answered that he had decided to run the experiment himself and knew it had been done correctly. The engineer finally agreed that location in the press made no difference. By examination, the investigator found that those pushed in too far had flash on the back, while those not pushed in far enough had flash on the front. The only difference caused by distance into the forge was the location of the excess flash, which would be trimmed anyway. The cavity in the die determined the dimensions and the operator did not influence the results in any significant way.

However, the engineer was still reluctant to accept the idea that temperature made no difference. Since the quality controller admitted that it had taken him much longer to run the tray of work than it would have taken an operator, the effect of temperature on the results was again examined. The data was replotted, comparing the first 10 parts forged (the hottest ones) with the "middle" 10 and with the last 10 (the least hot ones). Figure 23 shows the results with the top, middle and bottom readings averaged together. The figure clearly indicates that the temperature had no significant effect on the size of the seat even when the amount of cooling was greater than the

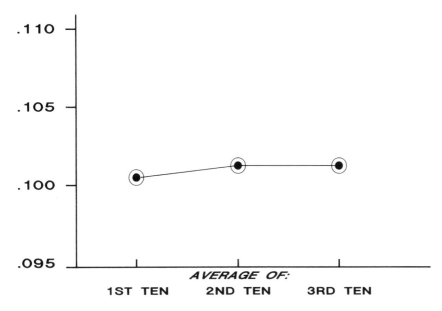

Figure 23. Average Seat Dimensions Show Little Variation even after Substantial Cooling

parts would have experienced when a skilled operator performed the job.

This case illustrates that "an ounce of data is worth a ton of opinions." The traditional Observe, Think, Try, Explain method did not work. To find the cause of the problem, the investigator needed valid data from a properly designed, carefully run and correctly plotted and analyzed key variable isolation study. However, even though the combination of a multi-vari study and a designed experiment eliminated the first two guesses—temperature and placement in the die—and zeroed in on the key variable—the size of the die—the implications were greater than that. In this typical factory situation, for example, if the engineer had been pressed for results, he would have responded that a few months and $30,000 later a new design would be in place and the problem would disappear. Unfortunately, time and money would not have resolved the situation. The procurement and installation of the two devices that the engineer wanted would not have corrected the problem, would have cost thousands of dollars and would have further delayed identifying the true source of the excessive variation.

CHAPTER 13

The Case of Bore Defects on Centrifugal Castings

While a problem-solving team was working with a foundry that centrifugally cast cylinder liners, the company's management asked the team to investigate a bore defects problem. The team first met with all key personnel and gave them the opportunity to suggest the causes of the problem. A meeting of this type is important because it assures everyone that management considers the solution to a problem to be a high priority.

The problem involved a visual defect which had not been previously quantified. Thus, the problem-solving team's first step was to devise a system for quantifying the defect. The team developed the following numerical rating scale:

0 — No Defect
1 — Minor Defect, Not Rejectable
2 — Major Defect, Barely Rejectable
3 — Rejected for Large Defect
4 — Rejected for Huge Defect

The Multi-Vari Study

Using this scale, the team then ran a multi-vari study. The company had six centrifugal casting machines. Three operators were employed to run these machines—each operator running two machines. The team inspected three consecutive castings from each of the six machines (i.e., 18 castings were inspected) at each of six different times during the day as shown in Figure 24.

While carbon content was one suspected cause of the problem, to intentionally change the carbon levels would have been a difficult task. Therefore, the team initially chose to simply record the carbon content during the multi-vari study. The intention of the study was to

OPERATOR	A		B		C		AVERAGE DEFECT SCORE	CARBON CONTENT
MACH. #	5	10	9	8	7	6		
1 9:15	0 0 0	0 0 0	0 0 0	0 0 0	0 0 0	0 0 0	0.00	3.06
9:30	0 0 0	0 0 0	2 2 0	0 0 0	2 0 2	1 2 1	0.67	3.19
2 11:25	3 2 1	1 2 2	2 2 2	2 2 2	3 3 4	1 1 4	2.17	3.43
11:45	1 1 2	3 1 2	2 1 2	2 1 1	1 2 1	1 1 3	1.56	3.43
3 2:55	0 0 0	0 0 1	0 0 0	0 1 1	0 0 0	0 0 1	0.17	3.12
3:10	0 1 0	0 0 1	1 1 4	3 3 1	1 2 1	1 1 3	1.33	3.34
AVERAGE DEFECT SCORE	0.61	0.72	1.11	1.00	1.22	1.17		

Figure 24. Tabular Results of the Multi-Vari Study

look for excessive within-casting variation, casting-to-casting variation, operator-to-operator variation, casting machine-to-casting machine variation, short-term time-to-time (five to 20 minutes) variation and longer-term time-to-time variation within the day.

Figure 24 shows the results of the multi-vari study. The three numbers in each block are the defect scores for each of the three consecutive castings. The column averages indicate that for all three operators the variation between their two centrifugal casting machines was very small, 0.61 versus 0.72, 1.11 versus 1.00 and 1.22 versus 1.17. The largest variation between operators was less than two to one, 1.22 + 1.17 (total, 2.39) versus 0.61 + 0.72 (total, 1.33). However, the average defect scores by time show great variation between the first two times (0.00 at 9:15 a.m. and 0.67 at 9:30 a.m.) and the next two times (2.17 at 11:25 a.m. and 1.56 at 11:45 a.m.). From these results the team determined that looking for excessive within-casting variation would not be useful.

The multi-vari study indicated: 1) insignificant casting machine-to-casting machine variation; 2) operator-to-operator variation of less than two to one; 3) large time-to-time variation and 4) defect scores correlating somewhat with carbon content—the higher the carbon content, the higher the defect score. However, these conclusions did not explain the variation between the 11:25 a.m. (avg. 2.17) and 11:45 a.m. (avg. 1.56) results when the carbon level remained the same at 3.43 percent.

Next, the problem-solving team focused on the significant time-to-time variation. The team asked what could vary within 20 minutes to cause such an abrupt change in the level of bore defects? At 11:25 there were two 4's and none at 11:45; at 11:25 there were only four 1's while at 11:45 there were ten 1's out of the 18 castings. The team felt that temperature was a prime candidate for the cause of the rapid changes.

The Designed Experiment

For the multi-vari study the problem-solving team had selected stratified samples and then had "let the process do the talking." The process provided two strong clues—that carbon content and another variable, possibly temperature, were causing the defects. The next step was to design an experiment in which the team could intentionally vary factors to test its theory. The team chose to run three temperatures—"hot," "medium" and "cold," which represented the center and extremes of the normal operating temperature range. The team selected five levels of carbon content, recognizing that it would be difficult to control the carbon content exactly. Concerned about other variables that possibly could change with time, the team randomized the order of running the 15 combinations of temperature and carbon content.

The importance of randomizing cannot be overemphasized. If the team had not randomized but instead had run all the "cold" metal first, then the "medium" metal and finally the "hot" metal, any differences in results would have been attributed to differences in metal temperatures when it could have been some unknown factor varying with time. Some engineers resist the need for randomizing. For instance, when running tests with varying temperatures there is a great temptation not to randomize because of the extra time it takes to change to the new temperature, particularly to a lower temperature.

The team chose to run three consecutive castings in each block to look at casting-to-casting variation. It made sense to take more than one casting at each level because it took so long to stabilize each condition. (Statistically speaking, these three castings were repeats, not true replications, because they were selected consecutively and were not produced by returning to the same set of conditions three times.)

Figure 25 shows the data from the designed experiment. As the carbon content increased from 3.06 percent to 3.19 percent, the average defect score increased from 0.33 to 1.22, a fourfold increase. However, as the temperature increased from "cold" to "hot," the average defect score increased from 0.00 to 1.33. This data indicated

CARBON CONTENT	METAL TEMPERATURE			AVERAGE DEFECT SCORE
	HOT	MEDIUM	COLD	
3.06	1 1 1	0 0 0	0 0 0	0.33
3.08	1 0 2	0 0 0	0 0 0	0.33
3.12	0 1 1	0 2 2	0 0 0	0.67
3.17	2 2 1	1 2 0	0 0 0	0.89
3.19	1 3 3	1 2 1	0 0 0	1.22
AVERAGE DEFECT SCORE	1.33	0.73	0	

Figure 25. Results of the Designed Experiment

that going from "cold" to "hot" (within the range of testing) had a much greater effect on defect score than going from a low percentage of carbon to a high percentage of carbon (within the range of testing). From these two conclusions, an investigator might assume that high temperature/high carbon was the worst condition, and, indeed, the lower left corner of Figure 25 is the worst block. Also, it might be assumed that the best block would be the low temperature/low carbon block and, in fact, the upper right corner of Figure 25 is all 0's. However, all 0's appear not only in the upper right corner but in the entire right column where the temperature was "cold." In addition to depicting the effects of carbon level and temperature, this visual analysis provided a third conclusion. If the metal was poured "cold" enough, carbon (within the range of testing) did not have an effect on the defect score. To describe the effect of carbon content on the defect score the team had to say, "It depends on the temperature," which means that an interaction was involved.

There were a number of practical implications to understanding the

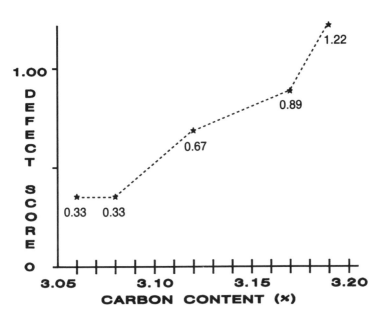

Figure 26. Average Defect Scores Vs. Carbon Level

two key variables, carbon content and temperature, and also the interaction between them. The team concluded that the problem could be solved by keeping both temperature and carbon content low. On the other hand, the process could be made less sensitive to variation in carbon content with better temperature control—and temperature was easier to control than carbon content.

Summary

For further clarification, Figures 26 and 27 show the main effects of the key variables, carbon content and temperature, each plotted on the same average defect score scale. Note that the plots of both of the graphs increase from lower left to upper right, further indicating that defect scores increase as temperature and carbon content increase.

The effect of the interaction between carbon content and temperature on the defect level is shown in Figure 28. This figure

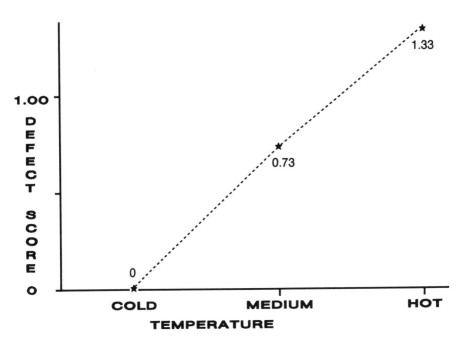

Figure 27. Average Defect Scores Vs. Metal Temperature

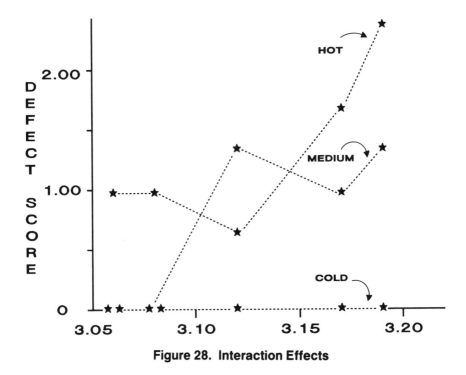

Figure 28. Interaction Effects

uses the data derived from the averages of the three-piece individual-defect scores shown in Figure 25. Note that the plots of the defect levels for the medium and hot temperatures are erratic and tend to slope upwards while the plot of the defect levels at the low temperature is a horizontal line at zero defects. Figure 28 reflects a non-parallel response. A non-parallel response indicates the presence of an interaction.

CHAPTER 14

The Case of Weeping Stoppers

By Thomas S. Woods

A Pareto analysis had shown that leaks were the most serious defects in the molded stoppers which a company manufactured. These stoppers were made of a new type of material, and, if the incidence of leaks could be reduced substantially, the company had high hopes for the success of the product. A management task force assigned to solve the leak problem decided to use the key variable isolation strategy and named a three-person team to undertake the job. The team included the design engineer for the project, the production supervisor and a process engineer.

Stoppers were first tested under "field conditions." During this testing, the stoppers were inserted into a circular glass opening of a special container, simulating the neck of a bottle. Pressure then was applied to a liquid inside the container, and the team observed the neck and stopper to see if any drops of liquid escaped. Stoppers that showed drops, or "tears," were referred to as "weepers." Although this method was adequate for determining whether a given stopper leaked, it did not provide sufficient information about the severity of an individual leak so that the team could discriminate between various levels of leakers.

To obtain more information about the stoppers, the team tried several methods of improving quantification. Quantification is crucial to solving problems of this nature—it is extremely difficult to analyze data when most of the scores are zero. Eventually, the team settled on a multi-vari study involving overstress testing, which used a level of liquid pressure higher than that used in the first test. When defect rates are low, overstress testing can be useful. For the overstress testing, the liquid inside the container was colored red so that the team could measure the area of the red stain which appeared on a piece of white blotting paper applied to the outside of the stopper. The overstress test provided a distribution of scores, and patterns of variation soon became apparent.

The Multi-Vari Study

The multi-vari study showed that the variation in the amount of leakage past the stopper was greatest between stoppers molded in successive cycles of the same mold. The team agreed with the design engineer that the variables which fit the "cycle-to-cycle" category were material plasticity, mold temperature and the amount of stearate lubricant used. Each of these variables had been investigated individually in a number of previous experiments but the results generally had been inconclusive. Moreover, when these experiments were repeated, the results often turned out to be entirely different from the results achieved the first time. However, the engineer hoped that the current testing might reveal some new information.

At first, the location of the leaks appeared to be random with respect to the orientation of the stopper. However, when the location of every leak was plotted on a measles chart of the mold, it appeared that nearly two-thirds of the leaks occurred in the portion of each stopper that was made opposite the inlet where the molten plastic was injected into each cavity. Closer examination of the worst leakers then showed that the location of the leak was sometimes associated with the location of a nearly invisible "knit line" or seam in the stopper where the melted plastic flowed together in the cavity. When this knit line ran vertically along the sealing surface of the stopper (from inside to outside), it could provide a passageway for liquid to escape.

The Designed Experiment

Based on the analysis of the multi-vari study the team designed a three-variable, two-level experiment to determine the relative importance of each of the three variables—plasticity, mold temperature and lubricant level—on leakage. The first step of this experiment was to lay out the experimental design as shown in Figure 29 and to determine the two levels of operation for each variable. These levels were set to represent conditions near the extreme high and low levels of typical operation for each variable. Variable A, plasticity, was given a value of 7 for "low" and 12 for "high." Variable B, mold temperature, was set at 300 degrees for

PLASTICITY A			
"7" −		"12" +	
LUBRICANT LEVEL C		LUBRICANT LEVEL C	
NORMAL −	HIGH +	NORMAL −	HIGH +
300° − CELL 1	CELL 2	CELL 3	CELL 4
340° + CELL 5	CELL 6	CELL 7	CELL 8

(Left side label: MOLD TEMPERATURE, B)

Figure 29. Designed Experiment Layout Grid

"low" and 340 degrees for "high." Variable C, lubricant level, was set at "normal" or "high" levels of stearate lubricant based on the spray time.

The second step of the experiment was to determine the number of replicate runs to be made under each set of conditions. Because of production schedules and the time and cost of running the experiment, a decision was made to use the minimum number of trials needed to get a measure of interaction—two mold cycles for each of the eight cells, or sets of conditions, for a total of 16 cycles. (If the results of this "minimum" run turned out to be inconclusive, then a third and even fourth replicate could have been run at a later date.)

The third step involved determining the sequence in which the trials were to be run. Because there were eight cells (as shown in Figure 29), eight playing cards (ace through eight) were placed in a box and randomly drawn out one at a time to determine the sequence of the first run of eight mold cycles. The first card drawn was the deuce, so that the first cycle would be run under the conditions shown in cell 2. Cell 2 shows Variable A as (−), or 7; Variable B as (−), or 300 degrees; Variable C as (+), or high. When all the cards had been drawn, they were again shuffled, placed in the box and drawn to determine the sequence of the next run. The results of this "randomization" drawing are shown in column two of Figure 30. Columns three, four and five list the conditions for the three variables for each of the tests.

The fourth step was to make the stoppers. This step was done in the random sequence shown in column two of Figure 30, at the conditions shown in columns three, four and five. The fifth step was to test the stoppers. All the stoppers were marked and then randomized before testing, to avoid any systematic bias in the test procedure.

SHOT OR CYCLE	CELL NUMBER	CONDITIONS			RESULTS
		A	B	C	
1	2	−	−	+	17
2	5	−	+	−	15
3	8	+	+	+	17
4	6	−	+	+	25
5	7	+	+	−	13
6	3	+	−	−	16
7	4	+	−	+	06
8	1	−	−	−	24
9	6	−	+	+	12
10	1	−	−	−	21
11	4	+	−	+	17
12	7	+	+	−	06
13	5	−	+	−	23
14	8	+	+	+	26
15	3	+	−	−	20
16	2	−	−	+	09

Figure 30. Test Layout and Results of the Designed Experiment

Test Results

Results of the tests are shown in the right-hand column of Figure 30, and in the designed experiment grid shown in Figure 31. For example, stoppers made in the first trial run under the conditions described in cell 2 produced leakage with a total area of 17—shown circled in Figure 31. The remainder of the right-hand column of Figure 30 indicates the results for the other 15 cycles.

			PLASTICITY A			
			"7" -		**"12"** +	
			LUBRICANT LEVEL C		LUBRICANT LEVEL C	
			NORMAL -	HIGH +	NORMAL -	HIGH +
M O L D	T E M P E R A T U R E	B	300° -	24 21	(17) 9	16 20	6 17
			340° +	15 23	25 12	13 6	17 26

Figure 31. Designed Experiment Results Grid

The designed experiment was analyzed using an analysis of variance (ANOVA) program. The results shown in Figure 32 indicate that plasticity was not a significant variable and that although mold temperature and lubricant level on the average did not affect the amount of weeping, there was a strong interaction between those two variables (B and C). This interaction is plotted in Figure 33, first with mold temperature (Variable B) plotted at both lubricant levels and then with lubricant level (Variable C) plotted at both mold temperature levels. An interaction plots as a non-parallel response. In Figure 33, the plots intersect—an indication of a strong

FACTOR	SUMS OF SQUARES (SS)	DEGREES OF FREEDOM (DF)	MEAN SQUARE (MS)	F RATIOS	SIGNIFICANCE
A	39.06	1	39.06	1.091	67.2%
B	3.06	1	3.06	0.086	22.7%
C	5.06	1	5.06	0.141	28.4%
AB	0.06	1	0.06	0.002	3.3%
AC	60.06	1	60.06	1.677	77.0%
BC	189.06	1	189.06	5.279	95.1%
ABC	22.56	1	22.56	0.630	45.5%
Residual	286.50	8	35.81		
TOTAL	605.42	15			

A = PLASTICITY   B = MOLD TEMPERATURE   C = LUBRICANT

Figure 32. Results of the ANOVA Analysis. The High F-Ratio (above 5) clearly points to a B-C interaction.

interaction. (While in this case the two graphs actually provide the same information, in many studies "cross plotting" data can reveal important clues.)

To describe whether the mold temperature had an effect on weepers, the team had to say that it depended on the lubricant level. When the mold temperature increased from low to high the weeping score went down, if the lubricant level was normal. But the weeping score went up as mold temperature increased if the lubricant level was high (see the left-hand graph in Figure 33). This interaction was the reason the design engineer had obtained inconclusive results during earlier testing.

As Figure 34 indicates, the worst combinations occurred when the mold temperature was low and the lubricant level was normal (a score of 81), and also when the mold temperature was high and the lubricant level was high (a score of 80). The scores in Figure 34 are derived from the data in Figure 30. For example, the score of 81 in Figure 34 comprises the scores where condition B is (−) and C is (−) without regard for condition A. These numbers—16, 24, 21 and 20— total 81.

The team's conclusion was that running the operation at the low mold temperature (300 degrees) and at the high level of stearate lubricant would provide the widest safety margin against weepers. The second best combination, mold temperature at 340 degrees and stearate lubricant at normal level, would also provide an adequate safety margin against weepers. Either combination could be chosen depending on ease of operation and economic factors.

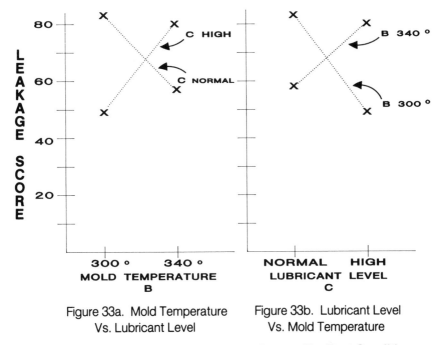

Figure 33a. Mold Temperature
Vs. Lubricant Level

Figure 33b. Lubricant Level
Vs. Mold Temperature

Figure 33. Interaction Plots — Leakage Scores Vs. Test Conditions

			MOLD TEMPERATURE B	
			300° −	340° +
L U B R I C A N T	L E V E L	C	NORMAL −	81	57
			HIGH +	49	80

Figure 34. Summary of Leakage Scores for B and C Conditions

CHAPTER 15

The Case of the Noisy Motor
By Art Leason

A top-of-the-line manufacturer had enjoyed high consumer regard for its product for several decades. With time, the product had undergone minor alterations as new materials became available and as the company's manufacturing concept changed and developed. The energy crisis and high consumer acceptance led to the use of the product in more critical situations than the designers originally had planned for. Eventually, complaints began to surface concerning a noisy component of the product: an electric motor. The complaints were followed by a slow but steady increase in warranty costs. New competition began to enter the field. After some months the effects of warranty costs and leveling sales were reflected in the company's profit margin.

The search for solutions began in the traditional manner. Company management questioned manufacturing and motor design about what had changed and what might be going wrong. Manufacturing responded by showing that minor changes, each one by itself seemingly insignificant, had over a period of time developed an almost totally different electric motor. Motor design insisted that if manufacturing followed the specification limits the motor would work properly. These specification limits, however, had not been followed to the letter for years. Thus, the stage was set for a war of words and much finger pointing. At this point the problem-solving team was contacted and began working on an approach that would resolve the situation.

The Multi-Vari Study

The problem-solving team began with a multi-vari analysis of the motor. As a part of the multi-vari analysis, the following numerical rating scale for the noise was created:
  0 — no detectable noise
  1 — barely detectable noise
  2 — noise clearly present but acceptable
  3 — noise too loud to accept
  4 — gross noise.
The investigation proceeded with noise tests being performed on eight motors in a row in the morning, again at midday and toward the end of the shift. Noise tests at those three periods were repeated the following day. The results are shown in Figure 35. The inspector who performed the tests said there seemed to be a difference as he moved around the motor and thus the noise appeared to move. However, the best that could be done at that time was to score the total motor.

Figure 35 shows a large unit-to-unit (i.e., motor-to-motor) variation, but little time-to-time or day-to-day variation. Unit-to-unit refers to motors made consecutively. It was believed that a within-unit (within-motor) score could not be obtained. This belief was a

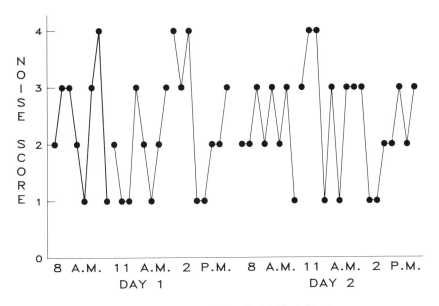

Figure 35. Results of the Multi-Vari Study

crucial flaw. If it is not possible to measure one of the main categories of variation, that category may identify the key variable.

The investigators agreed with the inspector that the amount of noise and its location within the motor seemed to change relative to the listener's position. The investigators then wondered whether, if the noise "moved" within the motor, could the noise "move" between motors. To answer this question, four motors at each noise level (1, 2, 3 and 4) were randomly presented to the inspector and were measured a second time. The results are graphed in Figure 36a. All the plotted points would have been on the 45-degree line if there had been an exact agreement between the measurement of each motor the first and second time. (This 45-degree plot is called an isoplot.) Instead, Figure 36a demonstrates little agreement between measurements. The same 16 motors were then given to a second inspector. In Figure 36b, the plot compares the first reading of the first inspector against the first reading of the second inspector. This plot does not show good agreement either. Figures 36a and 36b indicate that the same inspector did not obtain a similar result on retesting the motor nor did two inspectors agree on what the reading should be. The

PERFECT CORRELATION PLOTS ON THE 45° LINE

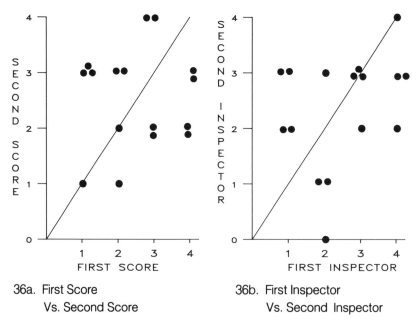

36a. First Score   36b. First Inspector
Vs. Second Score   Vs. Second Inspector

Figure 36. Isoplots of Noise Measurements

analysis is confounded between:

- Motor behavior (is the motor changing?)
- Measuring (listening) ability (frequency and amplitude variations)
- Other (interaction with other components such as motor mounting).

An attempt was made to train the listener/inspector. Repeatable and reproducible measurements still could not be obtained. Components such as bearings, armatures and brushes were switched but repeatability and reproducibility continued to elude the investigators.

Management agreed that the multi-vari analysis and isoplots clearly demonstrated the need for an improved measuring method. In addition, considering the amount of money being lost in warranty costs, management believed that it would make sense to invest in an objective measuring system if one could be found or invented. The project paused while a sound level measuring device was located and purchased and the investigators learned to use it. In addition, an anechoic room (an acoustically insulated room with low reverberations) was constructed to house the motor being measured. The measuring system consisted of the anechoic room where a motor being analyzed was hung from a TV antenna rotor in front of a sound spectrum analyzer microphone. The antenna rotor was used to physically change the position of a motor relative to the microphone. The motor could be turned through 360 degrees and an integrated sound measurement taken over 32 segments. The within-unit measurement then consisted of 32 segments of 11.25 degrees each.

When the noise measurement, anechoic room system was in place, a multi-vari test of the within-unit noise levels was performed on a typical motor. Figure 37 shows a plot of the noise level for all 32 segments along with a sketch of the motor testing layout. From the study, a clear pattern of within-unit variation emerged. What had looked like motor-to-motor variation was nothing more than the results of the random position of the motor in relation to the listener. The motor-to-motor variation was now resolved into within-unit (within-motor) variation. Some motors were slightly quieter, but the major variation was within each motor. The next step was to determine why there was within-unit noise variation. Then the problem could be corrected.

The potential list of a very large number of process variables had been cut by two-thirds through recognition that the primary type of variation was within unit—not unit to unit or time to time. The type of variation—within-unit—that was not captured in the first multi-vari study proved to be the one that involved the key variable.

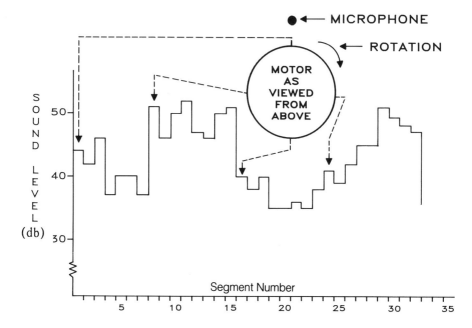

Figure 37. Within-Motor Noise Levels of "Typical" Motor

Evaluating the Clues

The sound spectrum analyzer used in the test allowed the investigators to measure a motor and mark a quiet location and a noisy location within it. After a motor was marked, it was disassembled and measured to find the "correlation of noise and dimension." Much to everyone's surprise, this dimensional analysis did not lead to an elegant and simple explanation of the cause of the noise. The within-unit clues found by the sound spectrum analyzer were confusing but did point to concentricity and the relationship between the stator and rotor as contributing to the noise problem. Therefore, an "old model" motor was constructed using old components still in customer service inventory and assembled using the old procedure as best it could be reconstructed. The results were spectacular. The "old model" was quiet and had almost no within-unit variation, as shown in Figure 38.

Dimensional analysis showed that the stator and rotor were smoother and more concentric than current model motors, information that the company already knew. The company had

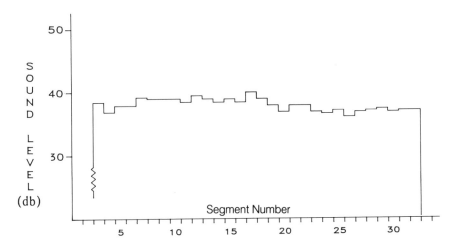

Figure 38. Within-Motor Noise Levels of "Old Model" Motor

previously made a decision to allow "rough" laminated stacks to be used in the stator and rotor in order to save money. This change had been checked and found to be acceptable. However, the method used to check the change could not be confirmed, as formal test reports had not been made.

Nevertheless, the clue that the old model motor was smoother and more concentric was pursued by building a very special new stator and rotor where concentricity of the stator to the rotor could be adjusted. This was accomplished by making small changes in concentricity in the metrology laboratory. The concentricity of the stator to the rotor is measured in total indicator reading (TIR). Figure 39 shows the within-unit variation with a stator where the TIR of the concentricity was adjusted to 0.0060 in. The average sound level of 50.0 decibels (db) was too high to be acceptable and the within-unit variation was significant. By using an improved stator alignment with a TIR of 0.0050 in., an improved sound pattern had an average noise level of 48.2 db. The press for improvement continued. A further reduction of TIR to 0.0022 in. reduced the average noise level to 44.5 db.

Figure 40 shows the results when TIR had been held to 0.0015 in.—the average noise level was 42.8 db. and there is little within-unit variation.

Figure 41 shows an excellent relationship of db (noise level) to TIR: as TIR was reduced the noise level went down. Not only had the

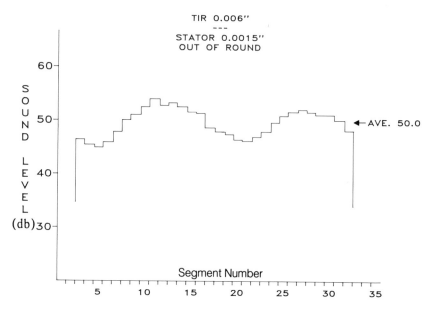

Figure 39. Within-Motor Noise Levels — 0.006 in. TIR

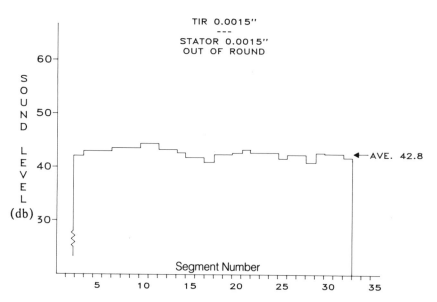

Figure 40. Within-Motor Noise Levels — 0.0015 in. TIR

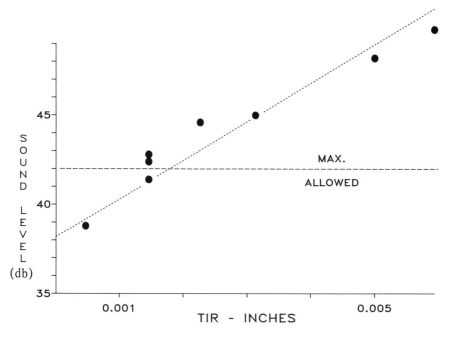

Figure 41. Relationship of Noise Level to TIR

key variable—excessive non-concentricity of the stator and rotor—been isolated but also a relationship, as shown in Figure 41, had been established indicating that the motor noise was a function of the amount of non-concentricity, as measured in TIR. The mystery of the noise had been solved. The results showed that when the existing specifications were followed, the motor was too noisy. This was a clear case of allowing specifications to grow more lenient until they no longer reflected the levels needed for customer satisfaction.

This case demonstrates the power of multi-vari analysis in problem-solving and the necessity of having an adequate measuring method. Multi-vari analysis provided a way to partition the problem, reject whole groups of process variables that had nothing to do with the problem and focus on clues that led to a solution.

CHAPTER 16

The Case of Random Balance
By John Pollard and John M. Reddy

A high-tech, "Silicon Valley" company making solid state devices was considering reducing operations at one of its satellite plants. The company had ample justification for this decision: profits had waned, competition had stiffened and management felt the need to back the winning operations and abandon the losers. In addition, the plant, while in relatively good order, did not meet the standards of the company's most critical customers. A prevailing belief was that at the very least a portion of the plant would have to be rebuilt.

Before the company made a final decision on the future of this plant, however, management asked a problem-solving team to review the operation. Following the strategy of first seeking out strengths upon which to build improvements, the team identified several pluses in the operation. The team found that the plant management and staff knew the technology of the process and the product. An eager work force operated the modern equipment efficiently and testified to their willingness to seek improvements. In addition, the company had a strong customer list. Many companies would find these enviable assets. However, the company's process yield typically ran only about 35 percent, i.e., for every unit shipped, almost two units did not meet specifications. Even with a highly favorable environment—no union, low labor cost, nominal overhead—this plant could not return a profit.

At the time the problem-solving team performed its review, plant operations were based on the following policies and beliefs that made it difficult to improve yields:

1. The root of problems lay in the operators not following

instructions. Therefore, only more training and discipline could improve yields.

2. Each day the company was required to review every operation for conformance. Any departure would automatically call for immediate corrective action.

3. It was required that proposed improvements be checked out one at a time.

These policies and beliefs might be useful if applied to some basic manufacturing operations, but this company's solid state processing involved 42 steps and hundreds of process variables. Normal processing time was about eight weeks. The idea of individually exploring the effects of improvements one at a time could not be used effectively in this complex process.

Random Balance

To approach these problems the team utilized a technique called *random balance*, developed during the 1950's by Dr. Frank Satterthwaite, a mathematician. Random balance is a type of stratified sampling that selects specific random paths through the process to examine the contribution of each variable. While this method can be complex in detail, following the random balance line of reasoning as it applied to this solid state manufacturing company's processes was a fascinating exercise in cryptography—much like the deciphering of a secret code. Dr. Satterthwaite based his reasoning on two basic ideas: sampling theory and the maldistribution theory (Pareto concept).

Sampling Theory

According to sampling theory, if there are major differences between items in a large lot, a relatively small random sample can determine the presence of these differences. The sample size is only slightly influenced by the lot size. Maximum efficiency is reached for a sample size of 30 to 50. A great deal of information is gained for each unit increase in sample size up to about 30, while increases beyond 50 yield a decreasing improvement in knowledge about the lot.

The purpose of a screening test such as random balance is to find the presence of any key variables, the effects of which, based on the Pareto concept, should stand out clearly. In the same way, if a random sample of combinations of process variables is tested, the key variable(s) should stand out.

Pareto Concept

The Pareto concept suggests that whenever differences exist there are one or more forces in action creating these differences. Even the slightest action, such as the arrival of the operator at his/her machine, has an effect—perhaps too small to measure, but still a contribution. The total number of variables contributing even the smallest amount to the total variation in a product can be very large.

Obviously, all elements do not make an equal contribution to the total effect. Experience supports this statement and, when the list of possible contributing variables is large enough, the effect of each contribution ranges from quite small to significantly large. Of the contributors only a few are generally responsible for a half or more of the total effect. Thus, the Pareto concept involves the maldistribution (unevenly distributed) principle. If all contributions could be ranked according to their effect, a Pareto chart, such as Figure 42, would result.

When the "effect" is variation, the Pareto concept becomes even more important. Well-known statistical relationships prove that

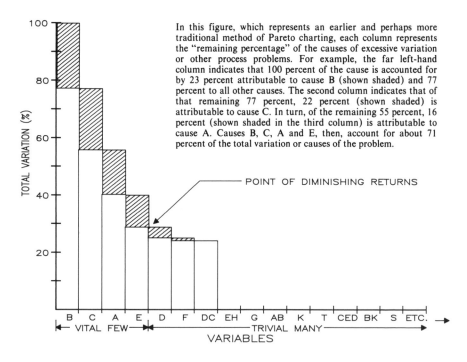

In this figure, which represents an earlier and perhaps more traditional method of Pareto charting, each column represents the "remaining percentage" of the causes of excessive variation or other process problems. For example, the far left-hand column indicates that 100 percent of the cause is accounted for by 23 percent attributable to cause B (shown shaded) and 77 percent to all other causes. The second column indicates that of that remaining 77 percent, 22 percent (shown shaded) is attributable to cause C. In turn, of the remaining 55 percent, 16 percent (shown shaded in the third column) is attributable to cause A. Causes B, C, A and E, then, account for about 71 percent of the total variation or causes of the problem.

Figure 42. Traditional Pareto Chart

random variation adds by the "sum of the squares" rather than by straight addition because it is highly unlikely that all variables will be at the level contributing the most (or least) variation at any given time. For example, using only two variables to describe the principle, if one variable contributes six units of variation and the second only one unit the total process variation V is:

$$V = \sqrt{6^2 + 1^2} = \sqrt{37} = 6.1$$

The major contributor has such a large, overriding influence that totally eliminating the small variable has an insignificant effect on the results. For example, if the variable contributing one unit of variation in the above example were removed the new total variation would be as follows:

$$V = \sqrt{6^2 + 0^2} = \sqrt{36} = 6.0$$

only slightly different from when the one unit of variation was also affecting the result.

A useful way to combine these two concepts—sampling theory and the Pareto concept—is to consider the magnitude of an individual effect, i.e., variation, contributed by each variable, as the elevation of mountain peaks, hills and bumps. In a region of few peaks and many small hills and bumps, if the highest peaks—"the vital few"—are removed, what is left appears relatively level and the removal of one more hill or a few bumps—"the trivial many"—changes the topography an insignificant amount. In real-life situations, this is the point at which the removal of the largest remaining contributor to the problem brings little practical benefit. It is often referred to as the point of diminishing returns. At this point, the removal of small effects does little to reduce the total variation. It does little good to locate and remove large numbers of small hills and bumps, if even one large peak remains.

By combining sampling and maldistribution theories Dr. Satterthwaite developed the random balance design for experimentation. His resulting strategy is a method for screening all possible significant contributing variables in a limited number of test runs. The strategy's primary objective is to locate the peaks—that is, the key variables—through a rough screening system. If 20 possible contributing variables were put into a random balance designed experiment, almost certainly the important peaks among the 20 would be located. It can be assumed that the maldistribution of causes of a given effect exists and that only a very few of the contributing causes have major effects while the large majority have minor and relatively insignificant effects. This assumption is borne out by considerable practical experience.

Random balance was developed from an earlier type of screening test, the fractional factorial designed experiment. However, to obtain the benefits of fractional factorials, the testing requires rigidity in its planning and execution. Also, it becomes difficult to keep the number of test runs low as variables are added and still keep balance, particularly when more than two levels of variables are needed. The fractional factorial design is most efficient as long as it requires 30 or fewer test sequences. Random balance does not have this limitation and therefore is more efficient when the number of variables to be studied requires more than 30 test sequences.

The random balance design does not limit the number of variables that may be programmed into an experiment. If 20 variables include all the "vital few" peaks, then it does little harm to add another 10 or so variables to the experiment since they must be in the category of the "trivial many." The real peaks will continue to protrude.

All significant variables should be included in the experiment to achieve the screening objective. Other unprogrammed variables will be reflected in the residual variation which the analysis examines. If the analysis is done sequentially, as the experiment is performed, test results will indicate the likelihood that any significant variables have been overlooked and permit the addition of newly suspected variables in the design after the experiment has started. Therefore, the random balance experiment—especially with its ability to add variables during the experiment—presents far greater flexibility than the more rigidly planned fractional factorial experiments.

Example of Random Balance

An example of a random balance experiment follows. The example involves a simplified situation in which the engineers believe that there are only six variables that are affecting process yield. Four of these variables, A through D, are to be tested at three different process settings (levels). The symbol "+" represents the process setting at the highest practical level that in the judgment of the engineers is acceptable in making a good product. The symbol "o" is used for the average level and the symbol "−" is used for the lowest practical level. For the remaining two variables, E and F, the engineers agree that testing only at the highest and lowest levels is appropriate. They decide on 30 tests.

The layout of the experiment and the results are shown in Figure 43. Note that test R1 is a replicate of test 6 and R2 is a replicate of test 19. The total of test runs in the example, therefore, is 32.

TEST LAYOUT AND RESULTS (YIELD)

TEST RUN #	A	B	C	D	E	F	RESULTS
1	o	-	o	+	-	-	58
2	o	o	-	o	-	+	38
3	-	+	-	+	-	-	04
4	-	-	+	-	+	+	92
5	o	+	+	-	-	+	73
6	+	-	-	o	+	-	76
7	+	o	o	+	+	-	66
8	-	o	-	-	+	-	28
9	o	-	o	-	+	+	56
10	o	+	-	o	-	+	08
11	+	+	o	-	+	-	69
12	+	o	+	-	+	+	82
13	+	-	+	+	-	-	78
14	o	-	+	o	-	+	71
15	-	o	o	-	+	-	46
16	-	o	o	o	-	-	44
17	-	+	-	o	-	-	02
18	o	o	o	+	+	-	55
19	+	+	-	+	-	+	24
20	-	o	+	+	+	+	61
21	o	+	-	-	+	+	44
22	-	-	+	+	+	-	92
23	+	-	o	o	+	+	94
24	+	+	+	o	+	+	83
25	o	o	+	+	-	-	66
26	+	+	-	-	+	+	54
27	-	+	o	o	-	-	16
28	-	-	-	+	-	+	30
29	+	-	o	o	-	-	64
30	o	o	+	-	-	+	71
R1(See #6)	+	-	-	o	+	-	75
R2(See #19)	+	+	-	+	-	+	26

Figure 43. Random Balance Test Layout

In this example variables A through D have three levels so to maintain balance there are 10 tests at each of the three levels. For variables E and F there are 15 tests at each of the two levels. Replicate tests are not included in the definition of balance. While the test layout is truly random, it is also balanced by maintaining the same number of tests at each of the levels. This is a form of stratified sampling which helps in simplifying the analysis.

Analysis of Example Test Data

After completing the 32 test runs a plot of yield was made in the order of testing to check whether any unusual pattern of results existed which might suggest some unknown, time-dependent influence on the test results. The test results were sufficiently random to ensure that no major unknown time-associated factors were influencing the results in any systematic fashion. It should be noted that the replication runs (6 and R1, 19 and R2) showed very good agreement when compared to the overall variation of yield figures.

A random balance experiment is analyzed by making scatter plots of the results. The scatter plots of the six variables are shown in Figure 44. Note that there are 10 points (plus the results of any replicate tests) shown in each plot for each test condition. The data for each of these points comes from the test results of each test condition shown in Figure 43. For example, each of the points shown for A− in the upper left-hand plot of Figure 44 corresponds to a result for which variable A had a low (or "−") value in Figure 43. To highlight the effect of each variable, the difference between the median readings for the two levels which produced the highest and lowest yields is marked on the scatter plots (see Figure 44). The four key variables in descending order of importance based on the numerical difference between the high and low median values and the best setting for each are: B−, C+, A+ and E+. From the data alone, the highest yields could be predicted, with reasonable confidence, by combining these four variables at the level which gives the highest results even though this combination was not tested.

Analysis of Solid State Process Data

Applying this random balance technique to the solid state process is somewhat complicated by the many process steps and length of time it takes to process one silicon wafer. The justification for all the extra work is that when 50 wafers are processed using a random balance design, it is then possible to decode the entire process and identify the critical areas for further exploration.

The initial test run in the plant in question included not six variables as outlined in the example, but 15 variables. The orientation and location of each silicon wafer in each process step was also recorded by the technicians. In addition, the electrical strength of each of the 200 or so devices on each of the 50 wafers was recorded.

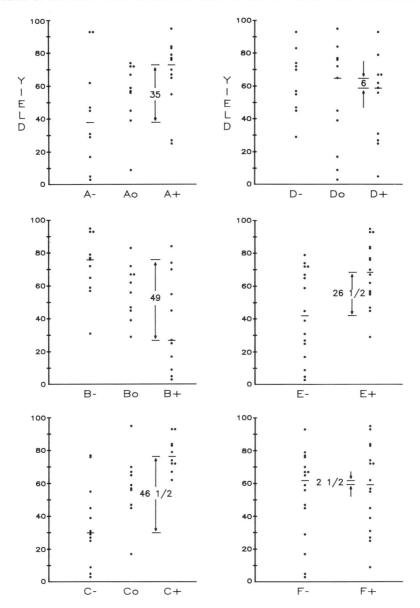

Figure 44. Scatter Chart of Test Results

The engineers could then observe the actual pattern of results within each wafer as well as the overall yield. The details of any random balance test run may appear complicated, but the process engineers within their own process are easily able to keep track of what happens. The engineers, after all, have lived with the many steps in even the most complicated processes.

Three trials over a six-month period showed exactly what had to be done to make consistent product. The answers did not relate to the work force, plant cleanliness or process upsets—the issues addressed by plant management. The solutions provided by the process itself revealed vast differences in the quality of incoming material. In addition, certain process equipment inherently could not make a consistent product, all of which was compounded by incorrect and incomplete specifications for several process steps.

The proof, of course, lay in the results of this process analysis. By implementing the findings from the studies, yields of 85 percent, rather than 35 percent, were realized. Senior management reversed themselves on the future of the plant and considered it one of their most significant assets. Plant management began to manage the process by consulting the process itself.

Multiple Balance

An upgrade of the random balance test design is a multiple balance test design in which groups of two, three or four variables are laid out in a full factorial test design while the remaining variables are randomly assigned. The way the variables are grouped is based on engineering judgment and past experience as to which variables are most likely to interact with each other. As with any screening test, using knowledge and experience is a great aid. With this strategy, the groups of two, three or four variables can be analyzed as full factorial test designs while all the other variables are treated as "noise" or residual error. As in the random balance designs, scatter plots are used to analyze all variables.

CHAPTER 17

The Case of Improving Aluminum Die Casting Quality
With Gregory Brown

A company wanted to improve the quality of one of its key products, an aluminum die-cast part used by the automotive industry. To achieve this improvement, the company decided to hire industrial investigators who were recommended by a major customer. The company was a preferred supplier, but the customer had become increasingly concerned about the quality level of the aluminum part.

The Quality Improvement Program

The investigators began their program for quality improvement with a one-day training session in the strategies and techniques of statistical process control (SPC) and key variable isolation. SPC training presented ways of using fundamental statistical concepts to measure and control excessive variation in a manufacturing process. Key variable isolation training helped the company's engineers to identify sources of variation that were missed by or unavailable to traditional problem-solving methods.

The program was structured around four long-standing problems that arose in the manufacture of die-cast aluminum products. These problems involved: 1) casting, 2) cleaning, 3) machining and 4) maintaining the plane of a faced surface. Teams of three persons from different company functions were set up to deal with these problems. Though the problems differed in terms of specific details, each was successfully tackled using SPC and key variable isolation strategies and techniques. During the training, the team members received extensive coaching and practice. This training allowed them not only to participate in and contribute to the solution of the four problems, but assured them the knowledge and experience necessary to solve, on their own, other product quality concerns.

Casting

The first quality improvement project dealt with the problem that had prompted the customer to recommend the investigators: too much porosity was present in one type of aluminum die casting when the castings were machined in the customer's plant. The improvement strategy called for creation of a numerical scale to rate the amount of porosity, a determination of the factors that caused excessive variation in porosity and a plan to reduce or eliminate the factors causing this variation.

A scale of 0 to 5 was developed to quantify the degree of casting porosity. Porosity scores were determined by the size of a wire that could fit the pores. With these standards in place, all subsequent castings could be classified and compared. The score also supplied the numbers necessary for statistical and graphical analysis. An experiment was designed to determine the effects of two common variables that affect casting porosity: fast-shot length and fast-shot velocity. Two levels of fast-shot length and three levels of fast-shot velocity were chosen to be tested during the experiment.

The designed experiment required the production of 12 separate castings, which were machined in-house in random order. After machining, the castings were carefully inspected and each of the six machined surfaces was rated according to the porosity scale. A measles chart of each casting was used to record the location and severity (0 to 5) of the porosity. Figure 45 is an example of one of these charts. To make the measles chart easier to read, the scores are shown on only two of the six surfaces (C and D) and only scores of 3, 4 and 5 are plotted. The circular casting was divided into eight sections to aid in the analysis of within-piece variation.

Results of the fast-shot velocity and fast-shot length experiment are shown in Figure 46. The main effects for the two variables are plotted using cumulative defect scores of porosity from the 0 to 5 scale. The plots clearly show that the fewest defects occurred at the medium level of fast-shot velocity. Fast-shot length had very little effect on porosity within the range that was tested.

Following the fast-shot velocity and fast-shot length experiment, a second experiment was designed to test the effects of three different levels of fast-shot velocity on porosity. These levels were the medium velocity previously tested, a little higher and a little lower. The objective of the test was to find the optimum level for the fast-shot

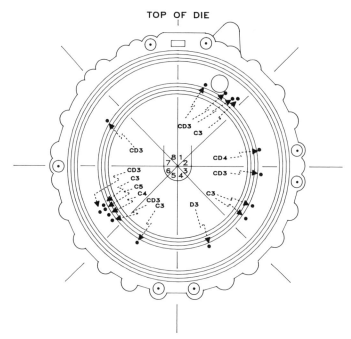

Figure 45. Measles Chart of Casting Defects

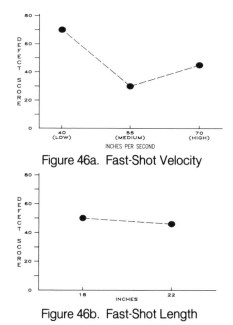

Figure 46a. Fast-Shot Velocity

Figure 46b. Fast-Shot Length

Figure 46. Results of the Designed Experiment

velocity setting. The investigators looked for this level on both sides of the previously best level. To ensure that the experiment did not exclude any other important sources of variation, pressure was chosen as a second variable.

The results of the follow-up experiment showed that the optimum level for fast-shot velocity was a point a little lower than the original medium fast-shot velocity level. Pressure, within the range of testing, had a negligible effect. Before the testing, there was a concern that porosity was related to the distance from the gates. The measles chart clearly demonstrated that the porosity at the gates was essentially the same as between the gates.

Where the optimum setting of fast-shot velocity was used, the defect level dropped drastically. It was now clear that while control of fast-shot velocity was crucial, controls over both fast-shot length and pressure did not need the attention they had been receiving. These last two specifications could be relaxed to save processing time and thereby increase productivity and save money.

Cleaning

The second project selected involved a tough cleaning problem. A large-size, large-volume aluminum die-cast part had strict cleanliness requirements for its interior surfaces, bored surfaces and internal holes. Before the project began, most educated guesses pointed toward the casting or machining steps of the manufacturing process as being responsible for "dirty" parts. Major contaminants—solder flakes, chips, dirt and foreign material—originated during these steps. At the end of the manufacturing process, 25-unit lots of die-cast parts were examined by sampling and were either accepted for shipping or rejected and recleaned.

The cleaning project started with a review of the cleanliness specifications. These specifications limited the size of the individual particles, their total area and their weight. The size was determined by removing the particles from the casting with a Freon flush, collecting the particles on a filter paper and then, with a microscope, examining the particles on the filter paper using a reference grid. Weight was determined by a "before and after" weighing of the filter paper. Since the weight specification had never been exceeded, the primary concern was to reduce the quantity and size of the particles.

As in the casting project, the next step required the development of a numerical scale to rate particle area and size. A scale was created, based on the overall visual impression of the particles as they appeared on the filter paper. To develop the scale, five filters were chosen to represent different levels of casting contamination (see

Figure 47). Each filter tested was then assigned a score ranging from 1 to 5 depending on which of the standards the filter most closely resembled. A perfectly clean filter, which never occurred, would have been rated a 0.

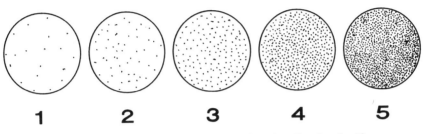

1   2   3   4   5

Figure 47. Numerical Rating of Casting Contamination

After the scale was developed, a multi-vari study was run. This study consisted of taking three consecutive castings following ultrasonic cleaning at two or three times per shift. The casting contamination level was rated according to the standards established. Important results appeared in just a few days. Figure 48 presents a plot of these results. The multi-vari study showed that casting-to-casting (piece-to-piece) variation and time-to-time, within-a-shift variation were negligible compared to the shift-to-shift variation that

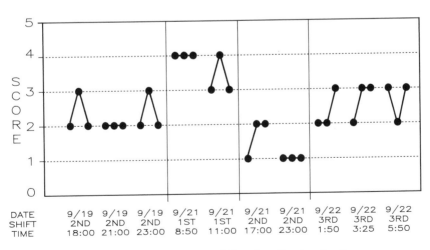

DATE	9/19	9/19	9/19	9/21	9/21	9/21	9/21	9/22	9/22	9/22
SHIFT	2ND	2ND	2ND	1ST	1ST	2ND	2ND	3RD	3RD	3RD
TIME	18:00	21:00	23:00	8:50	11:00	17:00	23:00	1:50	3:25	5:50

Figure 48. Multi-Vari Study of Casting Contamination

appeared. This result and the large variation that appeared between cleaning shifts clearly pointed to the cleaning process as the key variable. This was an unexpected finding, but one clearly demonstrated by the multi-vari data. Further examination identified several problem areas within the cleaning operation. Among these were that the washing water was not always kept sufficiently hot and sufficient wetting agent was not always used. The identification of these problem areas and the application of appropriate process controls to the cleaning operation brought casting cleanliness well within the required specifications.

Following the project, the simple filter inspection system to determine casting cleanliness and the numerical scale were maintained with a considerable saving in inspection time. Saving time was especially important because of growing production volume. Another result of the project was the removal of the lot-by-lot casting acceptance plan used prior to shipping and its replacement with a process control plan used at the end of the cleaning operation. This change virtually eliminated rejections and the saving in cleaning alone was substantial. Moreover, the customer received a cleaner, better product.

After a problem of this type is solved, it is often easy to say that better process control would have provided the answer. But this response fails to show how process control can determine which elements in the process are the most important and require the most attention. For example, before the study, process controls required frequent changes of rinse water in the ultrasonic cleaner. After the study it was found that rinse water changes were not important. Key variable isolation made it possible to identify the important and unimportant sources of variation in the process and thus determine where the greatest amount of control should be applied.

Machining

The third project dealt with a machining problem. One type of aluminum die casting had a very tight specification on the dimension from one hole location to the center line of a hole in another plane. The casting scrap rate for out of tolerance on this dimension on some runs had been 10 and even 20 percent. The problem-solving strategy called for the development of a procedure by which the hole-to-hole dimensional variation could be controlled.

Unlike the previous two projects, a usable, numerical scale in the form of a dial indicator reading was already available. Thus, step one was the running of a multi-vari study. To determine the major sources of variation, the multi-vari study examined the differences that appeared in the hole-to-hole dimension as a function of reading-to-reading (measurement repeatability), part-to-part, time-to-time within-a-shift, shift-to-shift and day-to-day variation. When these differences were graphed, it was clear that the most significant variation was shift to shift (see Figure 49). This result meant that one operator had a better machining technique than the other. Excessive variation was eliminated when the preferred technique was taught to the second operator.

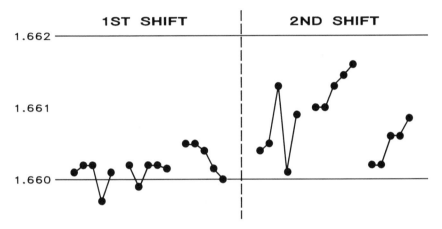

Figure 49. Multi-Vari Study of Hole-to-Hole Dimension Variation

Another concern involved the larger-than-acceptable amount of variation that occurred with the use of the dial indicator gage. This reading-to-reading variation indicated a lack of repeatability of the measurement. The problem was solved by purchasing a more precise (more repeatable) gage. One of the suspected variables, temperature, contributed insignificantly to machining variation within the range that temperature varied in the factory.

Following the identification of operator technique and gage repeatability (precision) as the key variables in this machining problem, it was important to ensure that these variables be controlled. In this case, a "pre-control" strategy* was introduced to guide the

*For a thorough discussion of pre-control see Juran, J.M. and Gryna, Frank M., *Quality Control Handbook* (New York: McGraw-Hill Book Company, Inc., 1988).

operator in making machine adjustments. Using pre-control resulted not only in better quality but also in fewer adjustments. The magnitude of the improvement was apparent when only two castings were scrapped in the next 1,600 produced. This level became the norm.

Pre-control is a sound, simplified method of establishing operator control of quality which:

- Indicates shifts in process centering
- Indicates increases in process spread
- Assures that the percent defective in the product will not exceed predetermined levels
- Assures that inspection frequency can be adjusted to an economical level, making it ideal for long production runs
- Assists with continuous improvement activities.

In addition, pre-control:

- Requires no recording, calculating or plotting of data. Plots can be made if desired. Thus, money is saved and it is more likely that the technique will be applied conscientiously.
- Can serve as a setup plan that starts with the first pieces produced. The technique is ideal for short production runs such as those often found in job shops.
- Works directly from the specification tolerances; data need not be accumulated to calculate control limits.
- Allows production to take advantage of the full specification tolerance. Pre-control does not try to control the production process more tightly than is necessary.
- Requires only simple instruction to use. Pre-control can be as basic as showing a "traffic light" comparison when the gages have been colored.
- Can be used with attribute or even visual characteristics. Pre-control was originally developed as an attribute control plan. A separate set of gages is used at the pre-control limits—the center half of the specification.
- Has as its target the center of the specification so that quality loss function is minimized.

Maintaining the Plane of a Faced Surface

The fourth quality improvement project focused on the evenness of the plane of the faced surface of an aluminum die-cast piston. Too many pistons were being scrapped because the faced surface was out of plane. An out-of-plane surface was determined by a two-step process. First, the castings were set on a three-point locator. Following basic rules of geometry, three points establish a reference plane. Then the contour of the surface around the circumference was measured in eight different places with a dial indicator capable of measuring to 0.0001 in. This measurement provided a set of distances that indicated the degree to which various points on the piston plane circumferences varied from the reference plane.

The eight deviations could be plotted on a clock diagram, which made it possible to compare the degree and location of out of plane from piston to piston. A clock diagram depicting a set of measurements is shown in Figure 50. (Note that had all eight points been in the same plane each point would have appeared on the zero axis—the dotted line—in the clock diagram.)

The next step was the multi-vari study. The study looked for the sources of the out-of-plane condition within piece by location, within piece from as cast to after machining, piece to piece within a cast lot and lot to lot. This information was obtained by comparing clock diagrams from the several pistons that were selected for measurement. The comparisons clearly demonstrated that the location of out of plane around the piston circumference was similar

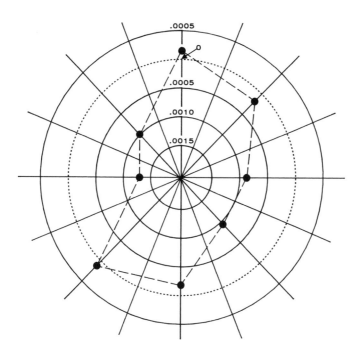

Figure 50. Clock Diagram of Piston Surface Variations

from piston to piston. This regularity strongly suggested that non-random sources of variation were at work in the machining step of the process. Supplied with this clue, the company's engineers scrutinized the machinery, in particular the chucking jaws.

What the engineers found supplied the solution to the out-of-plane problem. The chucking jaws did not apply an even pressure across the internal diameters of the casting and it was being "forced" out of plane. The engineers were able to document this deformation process by bluing the jaws, chucking a casting and then looking for marks on the blued surface and changes in the clock diagram. To further demonstrate the mechanics involved, a paper model of the piston was developed and stressed in exactly the same manner as the aluminum part. Surface out-of-plane deformations that were identical to those on the part appeared on the model.

The problem was solved by modifying the chuck jaws and their positioning on the casting. The jaws were ground to make them concentric to the center of the chuck. In addition, the width of the jaws was decreased so that they contacted an internal diameter of the castings in line with the main casting structure, a position where the casting is strongest. This solution provided additional benefits when it was determined that it could be applied with little effort to a whole line of aluminum die-cast pistons.

Summary

Application of key variable isolation and statistical process control enabled the company to solve four of its long-standing quality problems. This resolution led to products manufactured with greater reliability and at a lower cost. For the company, the advantages of these problem-solving strategies were:
- In-house scrap and rework rates were lower.
- Scheduling was easier because of lower losses in a run.
- Production schedules could be met more quickly.
- Higher quality, more consistent products were produced.
- Substantial savings in quality costs were obtained.
- Usable data was more easily obtained.
- Less frustration and better morale resulted.
- The company's technical expertise in die casting improved.

For the customer, the advantages were:
- Higher quality, more consistent parts.
- Better delivery schedules.
- Lower scrap rates.

- Dependable data when requested.
- A better relationship with the supplier.

The key variable isolation strategy as presented by the investigators proved to be a powerful problem-solving tool. However, the test of how well the strategy had been learned arose a few months after the completion of the formal consulting program. At that time, a major customer found that one of the company's products regularly failed an important quality test. The company's response was to apply the key variable isolation strategy it had recently learned. With this information, the problem was quickly diagnosed and corrected.

CHAPTER 18

The Case of Non-Disintegrating Tablets
By Charles L. Rosen

A major pharmaceutical company had developed a new product. This tablet had been on the market less than a year when the production department began to experience difficulties in meeting outgoing quality specifications. The product could not pass the standard USP (United States Pharmacopoeia) disintegration test, which required that six tablets disintegrate within 30 minutes in 37 degree C. water. If one or more tablets failed to disintegrate within that time, a second sample of 18 was tested, of which no more than one could take longer than 30 minutes to disintegrate. Failure of the product to pass this test and the resulting backorder situation were jeopardizing the company's new million-dollar product line.

Figure 51 outlines the manufacturing process steps for this product. First, raw material from an outside vendor was subjected to incoming quality control inspection. After inspection, the material was shipped to the formulation department where it was granulated, dried and then batched with binders and other inert materials. The product moved on to the compression department where it was formed into tablets and coated. After coating, quality control performed final inspection.

Because the product moved through two organizational departments, quality control and manufacturing, and two functional departments within manufacturing, a problem could escape solution because of unclear accountability. In this case, the manufacturing department believed that changes in raw materials and the test methods had created the problem. The department claimed to be doing all processing according to correct procedure and believed that the quality control department had not responded to a change in the raw materials. Furthermore, manufacturing believed that the quality control specifications were unrealistically tight and not indicative of the product's quality. They also suggested that quality control develop a test that more adequately represented the product's fitness-for-use requirements. In short, manufacturing believed that problem-solving efforts should focus on the quality control department.

On the other hand, the quality control department believed the problem lay with manufacturing. Quality control was reluctant to change test methods because raw materials had not changed a great deal and manufacturing previously had been able to make acceptable product. Another reason for their reluctance was that they felt the product with a longer disintegration time was not exactly the same as the product with the shorter disintegration time. If this were true, the government regulatory bodies could intervene because the company would be marketing a different product without approval. However, quality control admitted that there may have been a subtle change in the raw materials. A similar problem with disintegration had occurred about a year earlier and had been resolved after the vendor claimed to have changed his drying technique. Because the problems

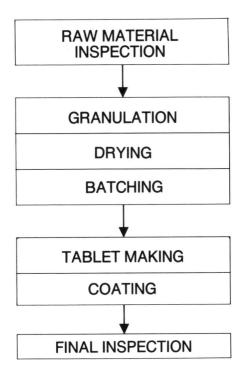

Figure 51. Tablet Making Process Flow Chart

appeared to be similar and changes in raw materials were on both the manufacturing and quality control list of possible causes, both departments agreed to have an in-house task force concentrate its investigation on raw material changes.

Tasks were assigned to both the manufacturing and quality control departments which focused on the raw materials problem but also looked into improved testing methods. The manufacturing department began an intensive effort to establish a better relationship with the vendor to see what could be done about improving the raw materials. Furthermore, manufacturing tried developing a use test to screen incoming raw material. This test involved making small batches of the final product in order to differentiate satisfactory from unsatisfactory raw material.

The quality control department concentrated on intensive analysis of all the accumulated data and contracted with outside laboratories to develop new raw material tests. In addition, quality control developed the criteria for easier release tests and was also prepared to do actual user tests to qualify product. However, after several months, the problem was still not resolved. Therefore, management agreed to have an outside team assist the problem-solving efforts.

Quantification

Existing records of the problem usually indicated only how many batches were rejected. In some cases, however, the records also included how many of the six tablets in a sample failed to disintegrate in the required time and stated the time it took for the last tablet to disintegrate. The problem-solving team plotted these results on control charts to examine trends, etc. From these plots, it became obvious that the measurement technique was inadequate for the purposes of detecting subtle changes in the product. A more sensitive scale for the product was needed—one that could detect when relative results, not simply rejects or acceptables, were being obtained. "Pass" testing only allows a decision of "pass" or "fail" and does not provide data that can be analyzed.

To begin, the team recorded the disintegration times for each tablet separately. Previously, when a batch had failed, it was not clear from the data whether it failed because the average disintegration time of the batch was increasing, whether the spread of the values was increasing or whether there were occasional outliers. The team proposed a more meaningful test—one that would be time consuming, often requiring an analyst to observe and record data for over half an hour. This test would also require more than six tablets per testing batch—30 or more tablets were chosen as a suitable sample size for obtaining data. It was not obvious how many batches would have to be tested nor how much useful data the test would produce. However, pressures to resolve the problem helped the team find an automated test apparatus and testing began.

The Multi-Vari Study

Assumption of a wide normal curve of disintegration time extending beyond the cutoff point of 30 minutes as indicated in Figure 52 was shown to be incorrect. It was, in fact, found that there were two distributions of disintegration times. The result was a bimodal distribution as shown in Figure 53. In some batches all

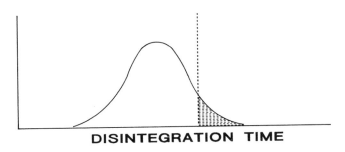

DISINTEGRATION TIME

Figure 52. Tail of Disintegration Time Distribution Extends Beyond Specification Limit

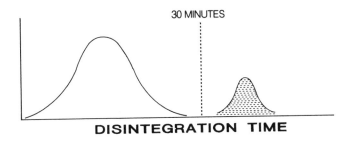

30 MINUTES

DISINTEGRATION TIME

Figure 53. Bimodal Distribution of Disintegration Times

tablets were acceptable and in all rejected batches most tablets were acceptable, meaning that regardless of raw material changes it was possible to make good tablets from all materials. Thus, the new raw material could not be the only cause of the problem. This observation proved critical and changed the nature of the investigation. The issue became one of discovering what factor in the process caused some tablets to go bad.

Samples were taken to identify where the variation was greatest. The main types of variation were found to be time to time and place to place. Time-to-time variation appeared as differences between consecutive batches made from the same raw materials. Place-to-place variation involved the difference between product made in the laboratory and product made in the factory. All tablets made in the laboratory passed the test and some batches made in the factory passed but some batches made in the factory exhibited the bimodal distribution of disintegration times as shown in Figure 53.

A bimodal distribution of results indicates that there is within-batch variation. In the past, the granulation process had been identified as a source of within-batch variation. The team now focused its attention on that process because there seemed to be considerable leeway in the operating procedures. However, the study found nothing to indicate problems either going into or coming out of the tablet-making process, a process much later than granulation. Therefore, the problem had to arise after that point.

The only process after tablet making was the coating process. The first product deviation from specification occurred after the coating. It was observed that tablets coated just before break time did not exhibit excessive disintegration times. Multi-vari tests were then performed on the coating process. Samples were taken immediately after the coating started, in the middle of the coating operation and at the end of the coating operation. The study revealed that if tablets were ultimately rejected, the problem occurred within the first two minutes of the start of the coating operation. If no rejectable tablets were produced during the first two minutes, there would be no rejectable tablets. Since the only part of the coating process that occurred in the first two minutes was the heatup of the equipment, this was a strong indication that the problem of rejectable tablets was heat (temperature) related.

During the coating process, the tablets were placed on a three-layer rotating drum, then heated, rotated and coated. The coater used for this product had a variable speed gear for rotating the drum—a low speed for heatup and a high speed for coating. However, the low-speed gear needed repair and required an operator to make a screwdriver adjustment at the back of the machine to enable the drum to rotate during heatup. Since the operating instructions ignored this matter, the operator often chose not to run the drum during heatup, but ran it only at high speed after the coating operation started.

The multi-vari study tested samples from the top, middle and bottom layers of the drum and found significant differences. The bottom and middle layers always produced good tablets, while the top layer sometimes contained rejects. Because the operators did not always rotate the drum during heatup, the tablets in the top layers often overheated and then failed to pass the tests. The immediate solution was to start the rotation and heating simultaneously. In addition, the mystery of "no rejects just before break time" was solved—just before break the operator did not leave the tablets in the drum long enough to overheat.

The Designed Experiment

With the knowledge they accumulated, the team designed an experiment to test the effects of time and temperature. In this experiment, tablets were heated in an oven to determine the effects of heat on the coating process. Figure 54 depicts the results. As the temperature to which the tablets were heated increased, the average disintegration time (and variation) increased considerably, particularly above a critical temperature. This critical temperature was the melting point of one of the lubricants used in the process. Replacement of this lubricant by one of a higher melting point could reduce the effect of the lubricant on the disintegration times.

A question still existed about changes in the raw material. Using a temperature versus disintegration time scale, the team now had a means of differentiating "good" material from "bad." The team found that the "good" material was crystalline and less heat sensitive while the "bad" material was amorphous and heat sensitive. However, all good tablets could be made from the so-called bad material if they were carefully heated and treated.

The cause of the problem turned out to be a three-factor interaction involving the new amorphous raw material, the lubricant and the method of operation of the coating process. All three factors had to be present simultaneously to produce rejectable tablets. The problem could be solved by avoiding the new amorphous material, using a lubricant which was not so heat sensitive and/or maintaining a close watch during the coating operation to avoid overheating the top layer. The permanent solution was to change to a less heat-sensitive

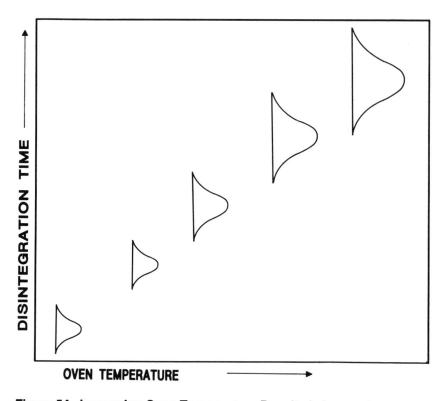

**Figure 54. Increasing Oven Temperature Results in Increasing
Disintegration Times**

lubricant. A remaining issue, however, was why the operators were allowed discretion as to whether to rotate the drum during the heatup cycle. The team found that the gear had broken about a year previously and the crystalline raw material then being used, which was not so heat sensitive, could make good tablets whether or not the drum was rotated during heatup. Therefore, rotating the drum during the heatup cycle was not considered important and was often ignored.

CHAPTER 19

The Case of the Mysterious Hot Crank

When a brand-new car is run until it is very hot, has the ignition turned off for a short while and then fails to turn over fast enough to restart, the car is called a "hot crank" car. (Definitions pertinent to hot starting problems are shown in Figure 55.) In this situation, mechanics and service station attendants may try various solutions to fix the car. However, the effectiveness of these solutions depends primarily on how long they take. Cooling of the engine is what actually allows the car to start.

The cause of the hot crank phenomenon eluded the automotive industry for many years. As engines grew in size over the years, starters became larger and more powerful. By continually increasing the power of the starter, the hot crank situation would abate for a while. Cold weather also seemed to reduce the problem and it could be forgotten for another year. However, the hot crank problem became critical at one major automobile manufacturer during the end of 1966 production (summer of 1966). The problem was complicated by the fact that there was no more room available for a larger starter. A redesigned starting system in the same space for the 1967 model year would have cost more than a million dollars and engineering management doubted that even this system would cure the problem.

These conditions prompted the manufacturer to ask an outside problem-solving team to join the engineering department to help resolve the long-standing problem. Five weeks later the major cause of the problem had been isolated, a correction instituted and the problem eliminated from production. Over the next few months, during the second phase of the problem-solving program, the team obtained more detailed engineering information to fully understand

Minimum Start Speed
The minimum speed at which an engine must turn to start and sustain continuous combustion. Typically, this minimum speed is about 40 to 60 rpm.

Hot Crank
The condition where the starter will not turn a hot engine at its minimum start speed.

Startability
The engine temperature (most simply approximated by oil temperature) at which an engine goes from a moderate to a hard start. This partly subjective measure has proved to be useful in identifying differences in engines. Two engines might both be hot crank problems but a startability measure can show whether one is more of a problem than the other. Investigation of the difference in engines can lead to identification of important variables affecting startability.

Hot Start
The condition where an engine can be turned in excess of the minimum starting speed but will not start. Carburetor, fuel pump or electrical components, for example, could be the cause of hot start problems.

Figure 55. Hot Crank Problem Terminology

the cause of hot crank cars. In the third phase, the team investigated additional refinements and longer term solutions at a reduced scale of effort.

Initiation of Study

The first step the problem-solving team took was to become acquainted with the hot crank phenomenon by looking at production cars that failed to start at high engine temperature. The most obvious problem with testing these production cars was the existence of an attribute-type rating scale in which a car was classified either as a "hot crank" problem car or as a "good" car. This scale was inadequate. Before the problem could be solved, and, in fact, before any test could be run, it was important to establish a measuring system that could be used to assess the degree of hot crank.

Another serious problem was the lack of repeatability in the measurement of water temperature at the upper radiator hose in relation to the incidence of hot crank. This measurement was used as an indication of engine temperature. The team, however, found that measurement of oil temperature was more repeatable and better represented the temperature inside the engine. Also, measuring oil temperature with a thermocouple at the bottom of the dipstick could be done easily.

Developing a Testing Procedure

The team proceeded to develop a test procedure, as shown in the example in Figure 56, in which a car was started and left to idle. A cover was then placed over the car's grill to prevent air from cooling the radiator so the temperature of the engine rose. When the oil temperature reached 201 degrees F., the engine was shut off for one minute, then an attempt was made to restart the engine. If the car started easily at that temperature, an E, for easy, was placed in the column labeled "Type of Start." The car was then allowed to idle until the oil temperature read 209 degrees F. Again, the car was shut off for one minute and a restart was tried. If this start also was easy, an E was placed in the 209 degree F. oil temperature row under the "Type of Start" column.

In Figure 56, the 201 degree F. and 209 degree F. starts were both easy and the 217 degree F. and 225 degree F. starts were

LOW LIMIT STARTER - 10 W		
TEST NO.	OIL TEMP. (°F)	TYPE OF START E, M, H, O
1	201	E
2	209	E
3	217	M
4	225	M
5	233	H
6	241	O
7	249	
8	257	

Figure 56. Example of Test Temperatures and Results

moderate (M). This car became a hard start (H) at 233 degrees F. and failed to start (O) at 241 degrees F. The team defined a numerical figure for startability as halfway between moderate start and hard start. The car shown in Figure 56 was halfway between 225 degrees F. and 233 degrees F.; therefore, the car was labeled with a startability figure of 229 degrees F.—a figure that repeated well on subsequent tests. The numerical figure identified a car's startability and therefore the team could measure the effect of subsequent changes to that car's engine.

Some cars did not reach a hard start within the range tested. Therefore, a higher pressure radiator cap was used to increase the boiling point of the engine's coolant so that the team could test above even 249 degrees F. All subsequent hot crank testing was performed with the higher pressure radiator caps. Some cars did not reach a hard start even at the 249 degree F. level.

Cars were "hot cranked" using this new test procedure as they came off the production line, with the team recording oil temperature and determining a figure which was labeled "startability." This startability figure could be used to compare any one or combinations of the seven variables the team decided to record for each car. These variables included 2- versus 4-barrel carburetors, airconditioning or no airconditioning, 9.9 or 10.2 compression ratio, 11- or 13-plate batteries, "Step II" (a more powerful starter) versus standard starter, battery specific gravity of greater than 1.240 versus lower than 1.240 and 20W oil in the crankcase versus 10W oil.

During the testing, a few pairs of cars were brought to engineering which were theoretically identical, but one in each pair had a very high startability and one had a very low startability. A component search test was made on these cars while other testing was continued and the data analyzed.

Test Results

The results of the testing were as follows:

• Oil viscosity turned out to be a key variable. 20W oil in place of 10W oil raised startability about 20 degrees F.

• The 13-plate battery was approximately 7 degrees F. better on the startability scale than the 11-plate battery.

• Batteries with a specific gravity higher than 1.240 were a few degrees better in startability than batteries in the 1.225 to 1.240 range.

• The Step II starter, which was more expensive, was not better than the standard starter.

- There was no difference between 4-barrel and 2-barrel carburetor cars.
- Airconditioned cars were not different from non-airconditioned cars.
- Because the data was unbalanced, the compression ratio effect could not be evaluated and had to wait for later testing.

Figure 57 is a plot of one of the component search investigations. The figure shows the startability of two cars, one of which had very high startability (250) and the other which had very low startability (192). This pair was selected because it represented the extremes in startability numbers and knowledge is often in the extremes.

The team made a total of 12 exchanges on the two cars. Prior to the fifth exchange, little difference in the startability of the two cars was noted. A substantial difference, however, occurred at test 5 in which the starters were "swapped." While the "good" car dropped about 10 degrees in startability, the hot crank car showed a remarkable improvement. In test 6 the starters were again exchanged and the test results returned virtually to where they were at test 4, proving that at least part of the problem involved the starters. The starter that

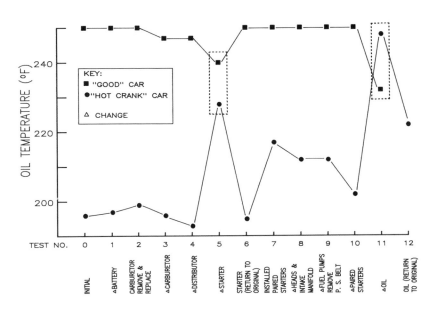

Figure 57. Example of Component Search Test Results

originally was in the hot crank car was sent to the supplier for testing where it was found to have two shorted coils.

Testing continued at test 7 where two carefully matched starters were used to replace the original starters. The result was a substantial improvement in the startability of the hot crank car and virtually no change in the startability of the "good" car. This result verified the role that the starters played in hot startability. However, something else was contributing to the hot crank problem.

Little change was noticed in tests 8, 9 and 10. In test 11 the engine oils were swapped and the results were dramatic. The hot crank car became a "good" car and the "good" car's startability dropped substantially. An investigation of the oils showed that the hot crank car originally had 10W oil in the crankcase and the "good" car had 20W oil. Putting the 10W oil back into the hot crank car (test 12) substantially decreased the startability, proving that at least part of the problem could be turned on and off.

The conclusion at the end of the testing was that the low startability car had two problems: a defective starter and 10W oil in the crankcase. Replacing the defective starter corrected part of the problem and changing to 20W oil corrected the rest. The component search study also revealed that further investigation of starters and oil was required.

The Designed Experiment

Next, five hot crank problem cars (low startability figures) were tested in a two-variable designed experiment. The two variables tested were 10W and 20W oil and low- and high-limit starters. Testing began by starting all five cars in random order with all four combinations of oils and starters. The 20W oil resulted in about 22 degrees F. higher startability than the 10W oil (see Figure 58), so unquestionably 20W oil raised startability. While the high-limit starter showed only a slight improvement over the low-limit starter, a later check showed that the two starters were, in fact, nearly identical in torque, rather than substantially different, as was the case with the starters in the component search test.

The team wondered if the same results could be obtained on a "test buggy" instead of in a car and also what would happen if other oils, e.g., modified 10W (commercially, 10W-30) were tried. Test results were repeated when the team tested five engines on a buggy using 10W, 10W-30 and 20W-20 oils (see Figure 59). The 10W-30 break-in oil was considered a substitute for 20W because engines would have to be stored and then used during cold weather. 20W oil, although effective for reducing hot crank problems, would have been undesirable under cold weather conditions. Results of startability

		STARTER	
		LOW LIMIT	HIGH LIMIT
O I L	10W	215.3	221.0
	20W	241.3	239.0

Figure 58. Results of the Designed Experiment

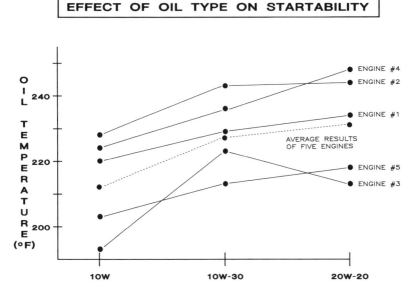

Figure 59. Results of Startability Tests — Engine Oil Temperature Vs. Oil Viscosity

testing showed that using the 10W-30 oil resulted in an average of about 82 percent of the improvement that could be obtained by using 20W versus 10W. Figure 59 shows the average plot of the five engines tested as well as the five individual engines.

The question of high and low compression had not been answered in the initial testing, and the effect of high- and low-limit starters had not been determined in the starter versus oil designed experiment because the "high-limit" starter was in fact not near the high limit. The effect of an advanced spark thus entered the picture. Therefore, the team ran another designed experiment, using a high- and low-limit starter and two distributors—one with a fixed spark advance of 6 degrees and one with a fixed spark advance of 13 degrees. The compression ratio was varied by using gaskets of different thickness. The resulting two compression ratios were 9.9 and 10.5:1.

Changing from the low-limit starter to the high-limit starter made about a 26 degree F. difference in startability. The difference made by changing from a 9.9 to a 10.5 compression ratio was under 4 degrees F., while the difference between the 6-degree and 13-degree advanced spark was only 1 degree F. and thus was considered not to be significant. Advancing the spark too much would make starting more difficult, but this advance must be 20 degrees or even higher.

Dynamometer Testing

During the testing period, the team set up a dynamometer to determine engine starting torque requirements. Engines were turned at 50 rpm for testing under simulated starting conditions. The most lucrative variable for immediate investigation was oil viscosity, so the torque required to turn an engine at 50 rpm at a temperature above 200 degrees F. was compared when 10W, 10W-30 or 20W oil was in the crankcase. Figure 60 shows that a test engine using 10W oil required about the same starting torque as when the engine was 20 degrees hotter and had 20W oil in the crankcase. All testing thus confirmed the 20 degree F. difference in startability between these oils. The 10W-30 again fell between the 10W and the 20W, but closer to the 20W.

In order to summarize the testing up to this point, the team developed a Pareto chart showing the main variables considered in startability and the effect or lack of effect each had on startability. This chart clearly indicated that the largest gain at the least cost involved using a heavier oil. To obtain a major increase in starter torque would be a great help, but this was a costly consideration.

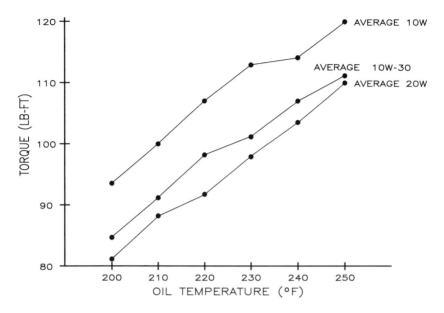

Figure 60. Torque Required to Turn Engines at 50 rpm Vs. Oil Viscosity and Engine Oil Temperature

With the major improvement obtained from the heavier oil, the purchase of the 13-plate battery would be well out along the scale of diminishing returns.

Analyses of the Testing

The thinner oil at higher temperature lost its lubricating ability and drained from the walls of mating surfaces. If the engine were restarted immediately, the oil would not yet have drained from the walls, while a longer time period allowed for cooling contraction and thus greater clearances between mating surfaces. Hot crank was most pronounced if the engine were turned off while hot and allowed to cool only a few minutes. Torque required to turn an engine at starting speeds is a direct function of temperature (see Figure 60). At running speeds the mating surfaces were in a bath of oil, and the viscosity was not an important factor. Torque requirements were not affected by oil viscosity—of those oils tested—in a running engine. Thinner oil such as kerosene allowed a hot crank problem below 150 degrees F., while 30W, 40W and 50W oil in the crankcase pushed the startability figure progressively higher, beyond the radiator's ability not to boil over, even for the most troublesome engine tested.

During testing, the statement was often heard that hot crank disappeared after "X" miles. This occurred because the starting torque required was reduced with use, that is, the engine was broken in. However, the value of "X" depended on the extent to which the hot crank problem had existed initially. More specifically, even though the startability figure increased (improved) with use, an engine with a very low initial startability figure could be a hot crank problem after many miles.

All of the team's testing clearly indicated that the hot crank problem was not an isolated phenomenon. Rather, it was part of a continuum on which, with high enough temperatures, "thin" enough oil, tight enough fits and/or a poor enough starting system (including a very low battery), the problem appeared. The hot crank phenomenon was really the tail of a normal curve where most of the engines produced were within the acceptable range. When the starting system did not equal the engine requirement, the engine failed to turn over fast enough to start. The testing established that the entire problem of startability might be looked upon as a balance. On one side was starter power and on the other side was engine resistance. Pumping the accelerator pedal often alleviated the problem of hot crank and got a problem car started because as the fresh gasoline emptied into the combustion chambers, it reduced the temperature and allowed the engine to start at a lower cranking speed. The cooling reduced friction and the engine thus was easier to start.

While there was concern that the startability testing procedure was inadequate because it used a subjective evaluation of easy, moderate and hard to define how well a car started, the degree of repeatability of the procedure proved its value. However, if a more precise measure had been developed, even smaller engine-to-engine differences could have been detected.

Before the 10W-30 oil could be specified for production use, cold weather testing was required. The test results showed that the 10W-30 was not as good as 10W at low temperatures nor as good as 20W at high temperatures.

Another previously unanswered question had been how much torque was required to turn the engine over at higher speeds with various oil types and at varying temperatures. Figure 61 shows that at 50 rpm the required torque was very responsive to temperature while at 500 and 1,000 rpm temperature had little or no effect on torque. An engine turning at higher speeds is in a bath of oil and the oil temperature did not have the same effect on torque requirements.

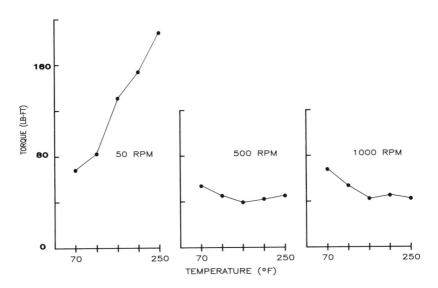

**Figure 61. Torque Required to Turn Engines Vs. Engine Oil
Temperature**

Figure 61 does not, however, show the effect of different oils. As
seen earlier, oils made a major difference under cranking conditions
at 50 rpm. The result of testing other oils at 50 rpm yielded curves
parallel to the 50 rpm curve shown. At the higher rpm's different oils
did not make any appreciable difference on torque requirements.
Therefore, torque requirements at 500 and 1,000 rpm were not
affected by the use of different oils.

The one remaining area to be investigated was engine-to-engine
variation due to initial fits of engine components. A designed
experiment was created with two variables of engine bearing
clearances and piston clearances. Two engines were built for this
experiment, one with tight bearing clearances and one with loose
bearing clearances and each engine had two sets of pistons built: a
tight set and loose set. Testing was performed at 50 rpm.

The results of this testing are shown in Figure 62. Engines with
tight bearings and tight pistons required much higher starting torque
than engines with loose bearings and loose pistons. The results of this
designed experiment indicated that startability differences could also

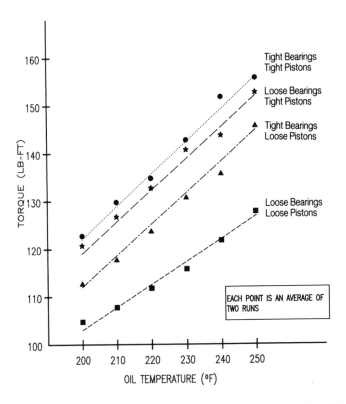

Figure 62. Torque Required to Turn Engines Vs. Engine Condition and Engine Oil Temperature

be caused by random variation within specifications for bearing and piston fit. This conclusion reinforced the importance of controlling process variables to the center of the specification and thus reducing variation.

CHAPTER 20

Variables Search

Variables search is a statistically based problem-solving strategy developed by Dorian Shainin. Like multi-vari, variables search is a rough screening test that directs investigation into important areas and eliminates unimportant ones. Before a variables search test is run, engineering judgment and manufacturing experience are used to determine which variables are likely to be causing the problem being evaluated, and these variables are listed in decreasing order of importance. (This technique differs from a pure multi-vari investigation where generally no assumption is made about potential key variables before the investigation is begun.) Then, for each variable, the investigator will decide which level of the variable is likely to give a "good" result and which level will give a "bad" result.

Before running a variables search test, the investigator randomizes factors such as test order, inspection order, raw materials, etc., that could affect the results. The investigator performs the first test with all the listed variables at the expected "good" levels and then a matching run with all the variables at their expected "bad" levels. These two tests are then run again to ensure that there is good repeatability. If the tests do not repeat well, there may be other important variables at work.

The next step in variables search is to run a pair of tests, the first of which has all variables at the "good" level, *except* the variable at the top of the list (i.e., the variable most likely to be a key variable), which is set at the "bad" level. A complementary test is run with every variable set at the "bad" level, except the top variable which is set at the "good" level.

The investigator then proceeds to exchange variable levels one at a time. This process of exchanging variable levels down the list proceeds until all the important changes have been made, i.e., the original differences between the sets of results have been switched from one column to the other. Then the investigator returns to the original all "good" and all "bad" levels and repeats the tests to ensure that other unknown factors have not changed during the time the tests were run.

Manufacturing know-how and engineering judgment are important parts of the variables search strategy. From a purely statistical standpoint, variables search and multi-vari are not as "clean" as some other statistical experiments, but they work well in the hands of competent practitioners. Criticism of multi-vari and variables search generally ignores the advantages of manufacturing and engineering expertise and common sense as adjuncts to purely statistical concepts.

The Case of High Scrap Rate on an Injection Molded Product

A problem-solving team had been asked to work on an injection-molded product that had a high scrap rate. This scrap rate, when combined with high material cost, resulted in significant losses. The scrap rate over an eight-month period was about 15 percent, with 3.6 percent being attributed to a defect called voids, and 5.8 percent attributed to a defect called surface splay. The remaining 5.6 percent was due to miscellaneous defects and the result of process start up. (Start-up rejects are inherent in the injection molding process during the period before the machine reaches its "equilibrium.")

The team decided to begin with a multi-vari study. Where the variables for controlling a process are not clearly understood, a multi-vari study provides a good way of reducing the number of variables that must be tested. In the injection molding process, 20 or more variables may be responsible for causing the problem. To set up a designed experiment with this many variables can be complicated and may not be successful. The multi-vari investigation in this case showed that the major type of variation for both voids and splay was time to time or run to run.

Correcting the Problem of Voids

A creative brainstorming session was held by engineering, quality assurance and manufacturing to determine which process variables might be responsible for the voids. Based on engineering judgment, experience and educated guessing, 11 suspected variables that fit the clues from the multi-vari study were chosen to be investigated. If 11 variables, all at two levels, had been put into a full factorial designed experiment there would have been 2,048 conditions to be tested. Traditional fractional factorials, Taguchi methodology and random/ multiple balance test designs also were considered but were rejected as impractical because of the large number of test runs and/or problems in running the required combination of variables.

Finally, variables search was chosen as the most practical experiment that could next be run and still be statistically sound. The team wanted to know if the most important variables were actually on the list of 11 suspected variables—the variables search strategy is an efficient way of making this determination. Once the variables search strategy was selected, the brainstorming group decided what the order of importance of the 11 selected variables should be and which level of each variable would give a "good" or "bad" result. This ordering is required to use the variables search strategy most effectively.

The level of each variable that was believed would give a "good" result was listed in one column of a table and the level which was believed would give a "bad" result was listed in another column. For example, it was judged that an injection time of 7.75 seconds was better than an injection time of 6.50 seconds; a hold pressure of 1700 psi was better than 1300 psi; and a hold time of 6.0 seconds was better than 3.5 seconds. The list of the variables began as follows:

Variable	Good	Bad
Injection Time (Sec.)	7.75	6.50
Hold Pressure (psi)	1700	1300
Hold Time (Sec.)	6.0	3.5
•	•	•
•	•	•
•	•	•
•	•	•

This list continued until all 11 variables were evaluated. The first test run was with all the variables at the "good" level. The second run was with all the variables at the "bad" level. It is necessary to repeat the original conditions to ensure that other potentially important variables did not change during the test. Testing then continued by changing each variable level, one variable at a time, in the order shown on the list.

At the completion of 23 test runs, including replications and capping runs to turn the problem on and off, three variables were found to be the most important. The total score for voids using the numerical rating scale was plotted in Figure 63 for these three key variables. For instance, the total defect score for voids when the hold time was 3.5 seconds was 950 points higher than when the hold time was 6.0 seconds. When the hold pressure was 1300 psi the defect score was 866 points higher than when the hold pressure was 1700 psi and an injection time of 6.50 seconds caused a defect score 656 points higher than when the injection time was 7.75 seconds. Of the 11 variables tested, these three variables stood out as the top three and explained the difference between good and bad product.

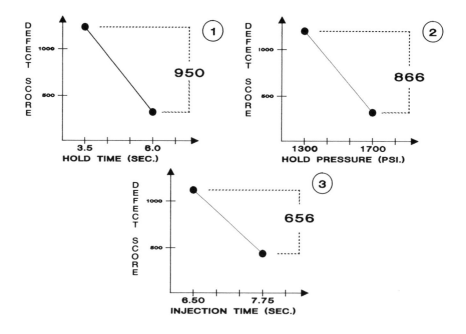

Figure 63. Voids Study — Main Effects

When many variables are selected for testing, it is a strong indication that the most important variables are not well understood. In this case, however, the brainstorming group did very well because the three variables were high on the original list.

Once the most important variables are determined, the next step should be to analyze these variables in a full factorial designed experiment. In this case, when the three variables had been determined, a two-level matrix of these three variables was drawn. This matrix had eight (2^3) test combinations, or blocks. With the 23 runs there was already at least one test result in each of the eight blocks. When more than one number appeared in a block, the multiple results were averaged and this average used as though it were a single test result. A standard statistical analysis (ANOVA) was made from the existing test results to further verify the relative importance of the three variables and to look for any existing interactions. If there had been any missing blocks, those blocks could have been tested and the results added to the matrix to permit statistical analysis.

Variables search is an efficient rough screening test and, when the results are properly analyzed in a full factorial format of the key variables, it combines test efficiency with statistical assurance. When the process was run at the correct conditions determined from the study, voids were essentially non-existent. When they did occur, the causes and corrective actions needed were obvious.

Correcting the Problem of Splay

The other major cause of scrap was splay. However, the frequency with which splay occurred suggested that optimum conditions for reducing voids would not reduce splay. This was not a surprise to the engineers because voids and splay did not necessarily occur together. A separate study was required to determine the causes of splay. After another brainstorming session, five variables were suggested as the possible culprits. With only five variables, a classical fractional factorial experiment would have been appropriate. However, the variables search strategy was chosen because of the success with the voids study, the low number of tests required, the limited availability of machine and mold time and the company engineers' confidence and enthusiasm regarding the method. After 12 test runs the top three variables in order of importance were determined and process corrections were made.

After the completion of the studies, the process was run at the conditions testing had determined would produce the optimum results, and the scrap rates for voids and splay were a combined total of 0.1 percent. This figure compared to 9.4 percent (3.6 percent for voids and 5.8 percent for splay) for the previous eight months: a 99 percent reduction in scrap for these two defects. In addition, the miscellaneous and start-up reject rate was reduced from 5.6 percent to 2 percent. When the major causes of defects are resolved, the frequency of defects due to other causes often is reduced because of the ability to detect and correct them more easily once the major causes are eliminated.

There were also some interesting side benefits to the solution of these two problems. When the problem-solving team had originally planned a program for the company there were two major aspects: equipment upgrading and statistical studies. Because of the success of the statistical studies in reducing scrap, equipment upgrading was no longer a major consideration, thus saving the company more money.

The Case of Low Pull Strength on an Electronic Component

A company's electronic component had been experiencing failures during an important quality check called a pull test. Because the component had been made using a complex manufacturing process, many variables were involved, and thus a problem-solving team determined that the variables search strategy was appropriate.

Thirteen variables were selected, placed in order of importance and the "good/bad" levels assigned by the key technical people involved in the engineering and manufacturing of the product. The first four test runs were made in the following order: all "good," all "bad," all "bad" and all "good." The consistency between the results of the two "good" runs and also between the two "bad" runs was excellent. However, the startling observation was that the results at the all "good" level and the results at the all "bad" level were essentially identical. This meant that the problem-solving team had selected 13 variables that had no measurable effect on the pull test results. The team then went "back to the drawing board"—actually, back to the assembly area and studied the assembly process more closely.

Subsequent investigation showed that the most important variables were related to assembly procedures that had not been considered on the list of the top 13. The variables search study had told the team that none of the listed variables was important. Any other test design, such as Taguchi methodology, classical fractional factorials or random/multiple balance, would have required many tests and in the end the conclusion would have been that the important variables were "none of the above." The team learned this fact in four runs. The engineers had been trying to tell the process what was wrong, but with the variables search study they were able to listen to the process.

Usually, the all "good" run gives a much better result than the all "bad" run and tells the investigator that the important variables are indeed on the list.

CHAPTER 21

Parallel Path Experimentation

Parallel path experimentation is a specialized form of component search or variables search. Like these techniques, parallel path is an important key variable isolation procedure because it narrows the area of investigation and moves rapidly toward identifying the cause of a problem. In component search, investigators switch parts of a product or machine to see whether a given problem changes with the changed part or stays with the unchanged parts of the product or machine. In variables search, investigators switch settings of a variable between "good" and "bad" levels to see if the problem stays with the unchanged set of variables or switches with the changed variable.

Parallel path experimentation is used when there are two (or more) production lines in a manufacturing process, each of which is producing a different quality of the same product. When one line is producing more defective product than another line, obviously something different is happening on each line. The parallel path experimentation approach attempts to locate the "bad" point in the line by sending products part of the way down one line, e.g., the "bad" line, then switching the product so that it completes the rest of the process in the "good" line. Simultaneously, products sent down the "good" line are switched at the same point to finish in the "bad" line. The question then becomes what will happen: will the "good" line become the "bad" line and the "bad" line become the "good" line, or will nothing change at all?

As an example, suppose during a parallel path experiment that the results (good versus bad) switch from one line to the other: the "good" line now produces "bad" product, and vice versa. Because the results are noticed at the end of the line, the investigator must therefore begin at the *end* of the line and work backwards, to find the defect-producing place. The investigator would move further back into the production lines and switch the product earlier and earlier until the point was reached where the "good" product turned bad and the "bad" product now turned good. At that point the investigator would have isolated the defect-producing station.

The Case Study

The following case demonstrates how parallel path experimentation was used to solve the problem experienced by a hi-tech manufacturer of semiconductor chips. At this company, production line 2 produced very "good" product, while production line 5 produced many defective products (see Figure 64). Using the traditional approach of Observe, Think, Try and Explain, company engineers reasoned that

Figure 64a. Semiconductor Processing

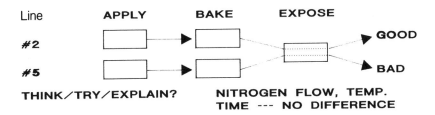

Figure 64b. Standard Production Sequence

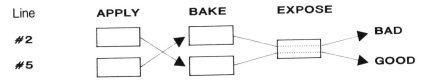

Figure 64c. Switched Production Sequence

Figure 64. Semiconductor Production Line Sequence

the variables most likely causing the problem in production line 5 were the nitrogen flow, the temperature or the time in the bake operation. Therefore, they conducted a designed experiment with different levels of nitrogen flow and various temperatures and times. Within the specifications, regardless of the different levels tested of the three variables, problems still occurred.

Management then asked a problem-solving team to work with the engineers to correct the problem and the team suggested conducting a parallel path investigation. During this investigation, the team decided to try the first switch after the "apply" step, so at that point the product on line 2 was moved to line 5 and the product on line 5 was moved to line 2. The team found that all the chips that had gone through the apply step on line 2 and then were baked on line 5 were good. In addition, the team found that some of the chips which had gone through the apply step on line 5 and then were baked on line 2 were defective. In other words, whether the product would be good or bad was not affected by the bake operation of either line 2 or line 5. However, the apply step in line 2 always produced good product and the apply step in line 5 always produced some bad product. The problem, therefore, did not lie with the bake step, as was previously thought, but with a prior step. A subsequent switch made before the apply step did not alter the test results, so the team concluded that the line 5 apply step was the key variable. As in the game of 20 Questions, the team had narrowed down the problem to the line 5 apply step. Any experiments on the bake step were bound to fail because that was not the location of the problem. Once the engineers knew the source of the defects, they were able to pinpoint the problem and quickly correct it.

CHAPTER 22

Introduction to Isoplots

An isoplot is a graph that can be used to compare two sets of results, numbers or measurements. The comparison of the two sets of data can be used to monitor quality trends, to audit the output of a process, to quantitatively describe the relationship between one variable and another, to evaluate problem-solving techniques and so on.

Creating an isoplot starts with gathering the two sets of data and arranging them in a tabular form. Figure 65 shows two hypothetical sets of data, called A and B, arranged side by side. The data in the left-hand column—set A in Figure 65—is considered the standard or reference data and the data in the right-hand column—set B—is considered the observed or measured data and is the data that will be compared to the standard data.

To compare the data on the isoplot, the two sets of data are plotted as coordinate points on a graph. For example, in Figure 65 the first pair of numbers is 1 and 2. To plot the corresponding point for these two numbers, one would move one unit to the right along the X-axis (the horizontal axis) and two units up the Y-axis (the vertical axis) as

A	B
1	2
2	3
3	4
4	5
5	6
6	7
7	8

Figure 65. Data Table

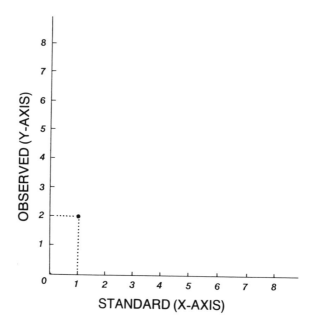

Figure 66. Plotting the First Point

shown in Figure 66. To place the second point (2, 3) on the graph, one would move two units along the X-axis and then three units up the Y-axis, as shown in Figure 67. The complete graph of the data in Figure 65 is shown in Figure 68.

A 45-degree line of perfect agreement (perfect correlation) is usually shown on isoplots. If the observed data were exactly the same as the standard data, the plotted points would fall on the 45-degree line; actual data, however, is virtually never perfect and virtually never plots this way. In actual use several types of graphs may occur:

• The plotted points may fall on a (more or less) straight line but not the 45-degree line, as is the case in Figure 69. In this case the observed data is referred to as *biased* or *inaccurate*.* This type of plot

*In this chapter, the terms *bias* (or *biased*), *inaccurate* or *imprecise* are used only to mean that the observed data does not agree perfectly with the standard. Because all "real-life" observed data is to some degree biased or imprecise, no attempt is made to define when data is *too* biased or *too* imprecise. That decision in actual practice must be made under the constraints of the use to which the data and evaluation will be put.

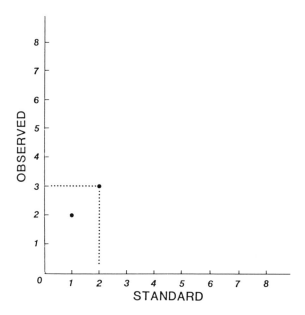

Figure 67. Plotting the Second Point

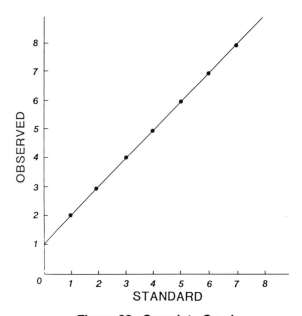

Figure 68. Complete Graph

often occurs when an uncalibrated measuring instrument, such as an uncalibrated micrometer, is used to obtain measurements.

• The plotted points may cluster around and on both sides of the 45-degree line as shown in Figure 70. In this case the observed data is often referred to as *imprecise*.

• The plotted points may "cloud" as shown in Figure 71. This type of plot results when there is no relationship between the standard and observed data or when the measuring equipment or technique is hopelessly unsuited to the task.

Using the Isoplot

Suppose that in an actual factory setting a scale of 1 to 8 is set up to evaluate visual defects on a product. Suppose also that a team of experts has evaluated 40 samples of the product and has agreed on a numerical rating to be assigned to each product item as shown in Figure 72. The company now wants to determine how closely the quality control inspector's numerical rating of these same 40 items

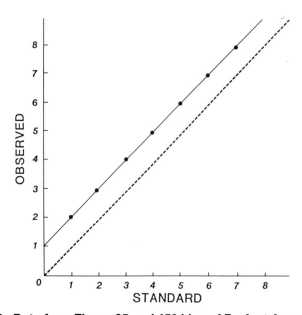

Figure 69. Data from Figure 65 and 45° Line of Perfect Agreement

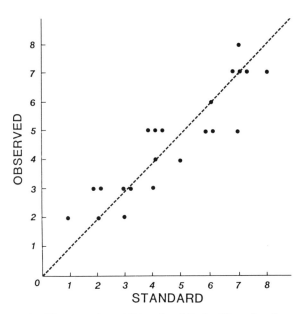

Figure 70. Observed and Standard Data Showing Imprecise Agreement

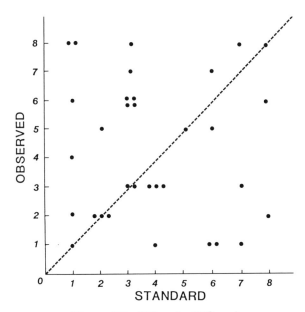

Figure 71. "Clouded" Graph

Item Number	Experts' Rating	Item Number	Experts' Rating
1	(2)	21	2
2	1	22	6
3	1	23	4
4	3	24	3
5	5	25	5
6	1	26	4
7	3	27	7
8	2	28	2
9	4	29	6
10	1	30	5
11	4	31	7
12	4	32	4
13	6	33	3
14	3	34	8
15	8	35	6
16	3	36	4
17	5	37	5
18	7	38	3
19	4	39	8
20	5	40	5

Figure 72. Experts' Rating Table

Item Number	Inspector's Rating	Item Number	Inspector's Rating
1	(3)	21	2
2	1	22	8
3	2	23	4
4	3	24	4
5	4	25	5
6	1	26	4
7	1	27	7
8	2	28	4
9	4	29	7
10	1	30	4
11	3	31	7
12	5	32	3
13	7	33	2
14	3	34	8
15	6	35	6
16	1	36	5
17	5	37	4
18	8	38	3
19	4	39	8
20	6	40	5

Figure 73. Inspector's Rating Table

will agree with the experts'. The inspector's evaluation of the items is shown in Figure 73. (Note that the item numbers shown in the left-hand column bear no relationship to the numerical rating assigned to the item either by the experts or by the inspector.)

The first step in creating the isoplot that will be used to compare the two sets of data is to arrange them in tabular form as shown in Figure 74. The coordinate points are shown in ascending numerical order. After the data has been compiled, the coordinate points are

Item Number	Experts' Rating	Inspector's Rating	Item Number	Experts' Rating	Inspector's Rating
2	1	1	26	4	4
6	1	1	12	4	5
10	1	1	36	4	5
3	1	2	5	5	4
8	2	2	30	5	4
21	2	2	37	5	4
1	2	3	17	5	5
28	2	4	25	5	5
7	3	1	40	5	5
16	3	1	20	5	6
33	3	2	35	6	6
4	3	3	13	6	7
38	3	3	29	6	7
14	3	3	22	6	8
24	3	4	27	7	7
11	4	3	31	7	7
32	4	3	18	7	8
9	4	4	15	8	6
19	4	4	34	8	8
23	4	4	39	8	8

Figure 74. Coordinate Point Table

plotted as shown in Figure 75. A typical point plotted is that of the experts' rating (2) and the inspector's rating (3); this point is circled.

Now that the isoplot is complete, a measure of the inspector's level of accuracy can be established by defining "accuracy" as the percentage of points on or within one division (as measured along the X- or Y-axis) of being on the 45-degree line. Of the 40 coordinate points, all but 5 are on or within one division of being on the line. Therefore, 35 out of 40 points are "accurate" and the accuracy rating is 87.5 percent. A more stringent method would be to count only those points that are on the 45-degree line. In Figure 75, 20 points would be on the line of perfect agreement and 20 would be off the line, a 50 percent accuracy.

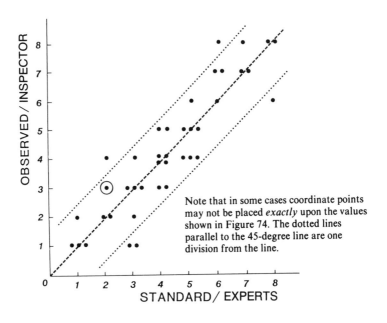

Note that in some cases coordinate points may not be placed *exactly* upon the values shown in Figure 74. The dotted lines parallel to the 45-degree line are one division from the line.

Figure 75. Isoplot of Product Ratings

A measure of "bias" can be determined by counting the direction and amount the inspector's readings are away from the 45-degree line and by summing the above-line (plus) scores, summing the below-line (minus) scores and obtaining the algebraic total. In Figure 75 this calculation is (13-12) = + 1. Dividing +1 by 40 results in a bias rating of +2.5 percent. If the algebraic total were a negative figure, there would then be a negative bias.

If a company wanted to determine how well a group of observers agreed with the standard/experts, isoplots could be made for each individual and the agreement then determined on a consensus basis. Accuracy and bias could also be collectively calculated.

APPENDICES

Multi-Vari Exercises

Introduction

The basic concept of multi-vari is straightforward. When a person faces a real-life problem, however, what to do is not always so obvious. Reading the preceding chapters of this book will provide the reader with a foundation of knowledge, but the true value of the book lies in the application of that knowledge to those real-life problems.

An excellent way of learning "what to do" is by evaluating either real-life experiences or "synthetic" examples. An advantage of a synthetic example is that a number of solutions can be built into the problem so that a number of teams can work on different solutions. In the following exercises, hypothetical examples assist the reader in learning "how to" apply multi-vari analysis.

APPENDIX 1

Multi-Vari Exercise:
Rope Consistency

The Process

Making polyester rope is a chemical-mechanical process. Various chemicals are mixed at controlled concentrations, pressures and temperatures to form a tankful of syrupy liquid plastic; the plastic syrup is then left to age in the tank for 24 hours under controlled conditions.

After aging, the syrup is squirted through hundreds of nozzles (a device called a spinnerette) into a chemical bath which, on contact, transforms the syrupy streams into solid streams, each of which becomes a filament or thread that will become part of a polyester rope. The rope is continually withdrawn from the bath at a controlled rate by a spinning line—a long train of wheels, some driven, some idling—that spin the threads or filaments into rope through a succession of rinsing, drying and conditioning stations. Driving wheel speeds, idler wheel torques, rinsing, drying and conditioning temperatures and times are some of the variables that can be adjusted to change the characteristics of the final product.

While the filaments are still partially plastic, controlled tension is applied to the rope to draw the individual fibers down to the desired diameter. The process is continuous, 24 hours a day, seven days a week, with shifts changing at 8 a.m., 4 p.m., and 12 midnight. Several tanks are used—while one tankful is being fed to the spinning line (a process of about six hours) other tanks are in various stages of aging.

The Problem

Control of rope weight per meter of length is important and weight is measured routinely at the end of the process by weighing, in grams, a 10-meter sample. The rope weight varies somewhat, but the loss due to excessive variation has become substantial in this company.

The task is to seek possible causes for this excessive variation.

Although many process variables are known to have an influence on rope weight, the question is which one (or more) of the variables (the **key** variable or variables) is likely to be causing the major portion of the variation observed in the end product.

The suspected variables include:

• Purity of any of six raw materials—some bought in small lot quantities, some in barge-loads. Each raw material has multiple suppliers.

• Precision of controls during mixing—such as rate of agitation, temperatures, quantities added, duration of agitation, cleanliness of tanks

• Controls during aging—such as time, temperature, pressure, viscosity

• Spinnerette malfunctions—plugged or partially plugged holes, extrusion pressure, viscosity

• Coagulation bath variables—bath temperature, concentration, flow patterns

• Post-bath variables—tension applied while plastic, rate of release of tension, speed of withdrawal, temperatures at the various stages, slippages on withdrawing wheels

• Measurement errors—sample length, scale accuracy, moisture content of sample.

Your task is to find out which one (or more) of the numerous possible causes is primarily responsible for the variation in the weight of the final product.

The Strategy of the Study

The objective of the synthetic example is to narrow the field of suspected causes: to be able to answer the question, "Is it animal, vegetable or mineral?" and then to further define the animal, vegetable or mineral.

The multi-vari study should rule out many "pet" theories and guesses and bring to light either a solution or reduce the remaining possibilities so that any subsequent designed experiments would have a very high likelihood of isolating the key variable(s).

The Multi-Vari Study

Assume that samples of finished rope were taken in the following manner:

1. Three samples were taken per shift for three days (3 samples × 3 shifts × 3 days = 27 samples).

2. Specific sampling times were randomly taken, stratifying them to be 3 hours ± 1 hour apart.

3. A sample consisted of 30 continuous meters.

4. Each 30-meter sample was carefully cut into 10-meter segments and weighed, using the standard laboratory procedures for cutting and weighing. This provides 81 pieces of data (27 samples × 3 = 81).

5. Four test experiment situations were tabulated, in three-day segments of time. Figures A, B, C and D illustrate the four complete situation results for multi-vari analysis.

Refer to Figures A, B, C and D. Study the plots, analyze them and write down your conclusions about the meanings of the patterns of variation. After completing the analyses, turn to the solutions to see how close your conclusions are to those given. For maximum learning benefit, do not look at the solutions until after you list yours.

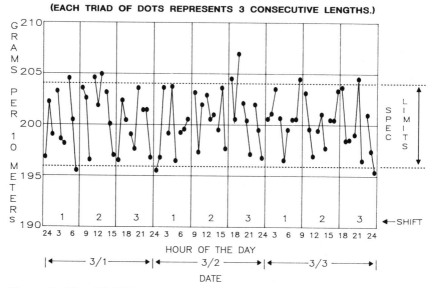

Figure A. First Multi-Vari Results

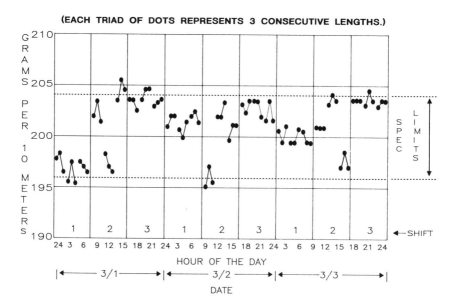

Figure B. Second Multi-Vari Results

140   Traver

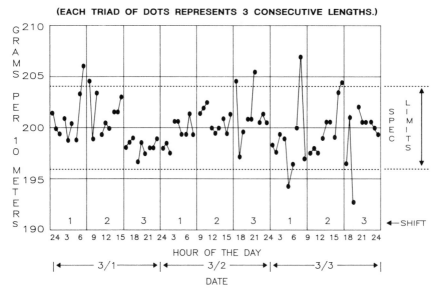

Figure C. Third Multi-Vari Results

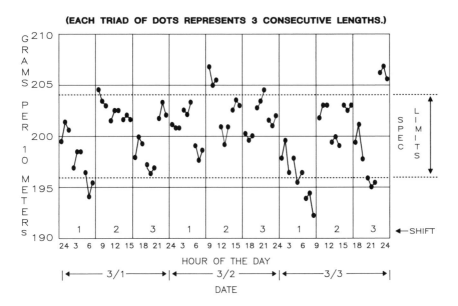

Figure D. Fourth Multi-Vari Results

Solutions

The clues and comments from the multi-vari plots are listed below:

Figure A

There is little variation day to day or shift to shift, and there is no consistent pattern within a shift. The major pattern of variation is the large differences in the three 10-meter segments within each 30-meter sample. This pattern of variation rules out almost all the expected variables, primarily leaving measuring or weighing variation. This lack of repeatability between the three 10-meter segments could be due to erratic cutting of the 10-meter pieces—perhaps due to stretching as they are cut. Perhaps the weighing device has poor repeatability. A possible but less likely cause is rapid erratic changes (within 30 meters) such as lumps going through the process.

The clues point to measuring, cutting and weighing equipment and/or techniques.

Figure B

The three 10-meter segments within the 30-meter samples are relatively consistent. The major pattern of variation is shift to shift. The second shift is erratic, while the first shift is consistent—although at different levels each day. The third shift is also consistent and is on the high side.

On the first two days when the first shift was not at the center of the specification, the second shift apparently overreacted by overcorrecting. One possibility is that the second shift is making large, frequent adjustments during its shift.

The corrective actions are related to finding why one shift is consistent and with a good aim, why one shift is consistent but high, and why the other shift is erratic.

Figure C

Starting on the third shift of the first day and continuing through the first and second shift of the second day, the process was quite stable. Therefore, it would seem conclusive that the process is capable of doing far better than it is now doing.

There were four times that a large amount of variation and out-of-specification product occurred. In each case, the problem existed over approximately a six-hour period. The fact that a tank of raw material lasts about six hours may suggest some possibilities to evaluate.

The second shift's average from day to day was more consistent than that of the two other shifts. On the second and third days early in the third shift, after the defects were very bad, the situation improved considerably. Did someone discover the problem and correct it? If so, capture this correction, make corrections earlier and explain the correction to the other shifts.

Six out of seven times when the process shifted enough to go out of specification, the results jumped out abruptly. Was the cause of the extreme change in results something like the spinnerette clogging and unclogging?

Figure D

Generally there is a lot of variation within each shift. The process usually drifts downward. On five occasions, when the downward drift was corrected, a large correction (often too large) was made. If smaller corrections were made more frequently, the process would have far less variation.

Apparently second shift cranks up the process when they come in, whether or not the process needs it. The second shift tends to run on the high side. Have they learned that because of the downward drift they can start their run on the high side and make fewer adjustments?

On all three shifts two of the three sets of data are similar and the third set is different. This is an interesting observation, but its connection to the sources of variation is not so obvious. It is a weak clue but one that may bear further observation.

Summary of the Four Examples

This study illustrates a complex process with many potentially important variables. Most designed experiments that might be considered would be very complex and difficult to run; therefore, it is important to run a multi-vari study to reduce the number of potential variables. Sometimes the clues from the multi-vari are strong and obvious enough to solve the problem or at least solve part of the problem. In other instances, the patterns of variation highlighted by the multi-vari study can eliminate most of the pet theories and their associated variables. Consequently, an experiment can be designed that includes only those few variables that fit the clues obtained from the multi-vari study.

APPENDIX 2

Multi-Vari Exercise:
Foundry Measles Charts

The Problem

A casting used in relatively high volume has experienced heavy losses due to porosity. Increasing customer demands will soon exceed production capacity unless a substantial reduction is made in the scrap rates. The customer is also pressing for a reduction in price, but the losses have kept costs quite high.

A task force composed of a foundry engineer, metallurgist, foundry superintendent and quality engineer has been assigned to solve the problem. The quality engineer, who is the task force leader, is experienced in key variable isolation problem-solving strategies. With the task force, the quality engineer has established a 0 to 4 numerical rating scale to rank the degree of porosity. The engineer has prepared a form (see Figure E) on which results can be plotted in a measles chart style with separate results for cope and drag. Two identical castings are made in each mold and are shown next to each other on the form. The task force decides to perform a multi-vari study to evaluate the porosity problem.

The Multi-Vari Study

The multi-vari study consisted of taking three molds (six castings) in a row around 7 a.m. and another three molds near the end of the run, around 9 a.m. By plotting the porosity on the measles chart the size of the defects can be shown on a 1 to 4 scale. Because cope and drag (explained below) results are separated, within-piece (within-

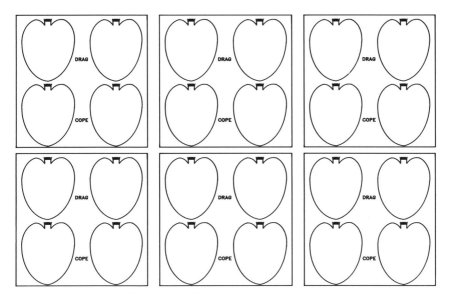

Figure E. Measles Chart Style Form

casting) variation can be measured. Since there are two castings in a mold, within-mold variation can be examined. In addition, by taking three molds in a row, mold-to-mold variation can be shown, and by taking samples two times during the morning, time-to-time variation can be measured. The task force decides to run the study a second day to look at the day-to-day variation. In foundries, day-to-day differences are often a major problem.

There are four different sets of results. These are shown in Figures F, G, H and I; each study reflects a different process condition, so each study should be evaluated separately. Figure F1 shows results for the first day of study 1 and Figure F2 shows results for day 2 of study 1. Figures G1 and G2 show the results for day 1 and day 2 of study 2, and so on.

In each square of the measles chart, the extreme upper left-hand heart-shaped picture illustrates the drag of one casting and another heart-shaped picture directly below illustrates the cope. The cope is the top half and the drag is the bottom half of the same casting; they are drawn separately so that the defects can be shown. The castings actually are lying down with the molten metal entering the gate in the *end* of the casting (the jagged part at the top of the picture is the gate; this gate is broken off after the casting has cooled). In the right side of the square is the cope and drag of the second casting that is poured in the same mold. The defects are shown as if the castings were "transparent."

Each measles chart is labeled so as to indicate day, time and mold number. For instance, in Figure F1 the label 1-7-1 designates day 1, 7 a.m., mold number 1. The next square to the right contains four more heart-shaped pictures representing the two castings in the second mold. It is labeled Mold 1-7-2 (day 1, 7 a.m., mold 2). In the third square to the right, the third consecutive mold poured at 7 a.m. is labeled Mold 1-7-3 (day 1, 7 a.m., mold 3). The bottom half of Figure F1 shows three more molds, poured at 9 a.m. (e.g., Mold 1-9-1 indicates day 1, 9 a.m., mold 1). The rest of the studies are numbered in the same manner.

At the top of each example is the defect score key for the measles charts. If the defect (porosity) is small (e.g., a "1"), there is a dot plotted on the measles chart. If the defect is larger (e.g., a "2") there is a circled dot. A "3" has a double circle and a "4" has a triple circle around the dot. In totaling defects (porosity) the numbers are simply added:

$$• \; + \; ⊙ \; + \; • \; + \; ⊚ \; = \; 7$$
$$1 \; + \; 2 \; + \; 1 \; + \; 3 \; = \; 7$$

Formulating the Study

For any of the four studies, day-to-day variation can be determined by totaling each of the two separate studies for day 1 and day 2. If all the 7 a.m. totals are compared to all the 9 a.m. totals, time-to-time variation can be determined. Also, mold-to-mold variation, casting-to-casting variation and within-casting variation can be determined. It is possible to plot the results in a typical multi-vari chart, but a simple solution is to compare the total scores for all the patterns of variation. (A multi-vari chart for study 3 is shown in Figure K.)

If, for example, the total score for all 7 a.m. readings of one study was 80 and for 9 a.m. the total was 40, you could then conclude that there was twice as high a defect (porosity) score at 7 a.m. as there was at 9 a.m. The next step would be to consider what could cause more porosity first thing in the morning—at the beginning of the run—as compared to two hours later at the end of the run. Causes of the problem might include metal temperature, sand temperature and humidity, operator alertness, etc. Each study includes more than one clue.

The "task force" (i.e., *you*) should review the results and decide which pattern(s) of variation stand out and by how much. Once these determinations are made, the "task force" should try to determine which variables best fit the clues.

Assignment

Your assignment is to review the four studies on the following pages to determine which patterns of variation stand out and by how much. Then, consider what might be done next.

DEFECT SCORE KEY: 1 = • 2 = ⊙ 3 = ◉ 4 = ◎

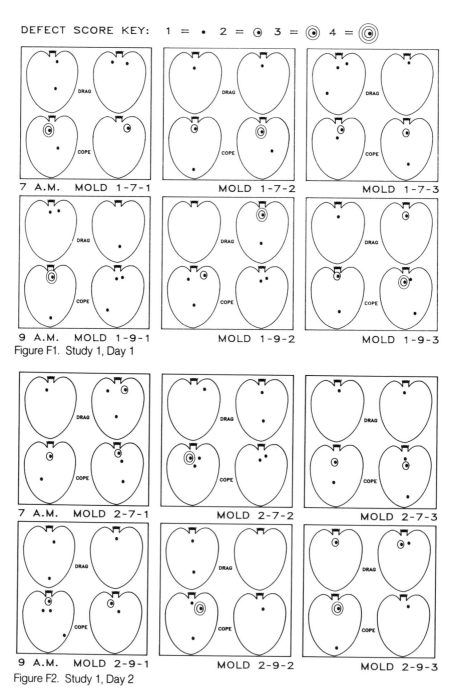

7 A.M. MOLD 1-7-1   MOLD 1-7-2   MOLD 1-7-3

9 A.M. MOLD 1-9-1   MOLD 1-9-2   MOLD 1-9-3
Figure F1. Study 1, Day 1

7 A.M. MOLD 2-7-1   MOLD 2-7-2   MOLD 2-7-3

9 A.M. MOLD 2-9-1   MOLD 2-9-2   MOLD 2-9-3
Figure F2. Study 1, Day 2

Figure F. Casting Porosity Study 1

148   Traver

DEFECT SCORE KEY: 1 = • 2 = ⊙ 3 = ◉ 4 = ◎

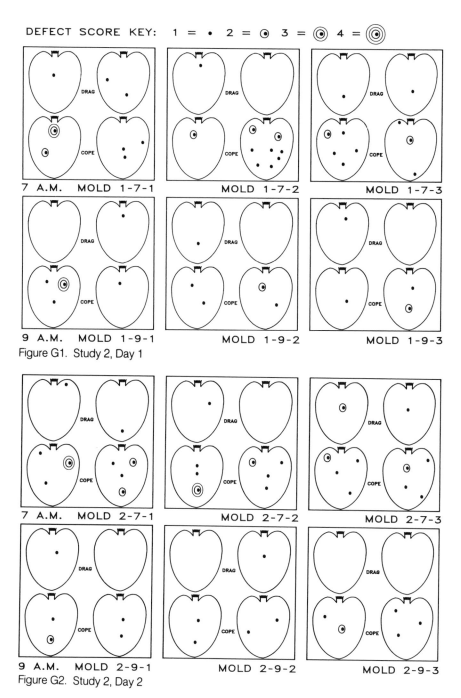

7 A.M.   MOLD 1-7-1   MOLD 1-7-2   MOLD 1-7-3

9 A.M.   MOLD 1-9-1   MOLD 1-9-2   MOLD 1-9-3
Figure G1. Study 2, Day 1

7 A.M.   MOLD 2-7-1   MOLD 2-7-2   MOLD 2-7-3

9 A.M.   MOLD 2-9-1   MOLD 2-9-2   MOLD 2-9-3
Figure G2. Study 2, Day 2

Figure G. Casting Porosity Study 2

DEFECT SCORE KEY: 1 = •   2 = ⊙   3 = ◉   4 = ◎

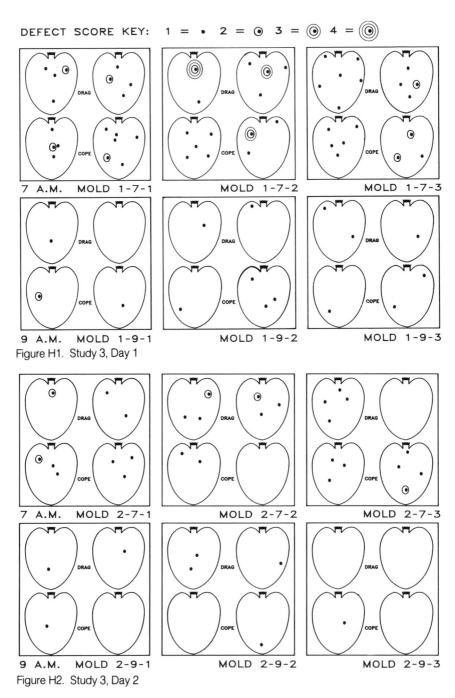

7 A.M.   MOLD 1-7-1   MOLD 1-7-2   MOLD 1-7-3

9 A.M.   MOLD 1-9-1   MOLD 1-9-2   MOLD 1-9-3

Figure H1. Study 3, Day 1

7 A.M.   MOLD 2-7-1   MOLD 2-7-2   MOLD 2-7-3

9 A.M.   MOLD 2-9-1   MOLD 2-9-2   MOLD 2-9-3

Figure H2. Study 3, Day 2

Figure H. Casting Porosity Study 3

150   Traver

DEFECT SCORE KEY: 1 = • 2 = ⊙ 3 = ⊚ 4 = ⊛

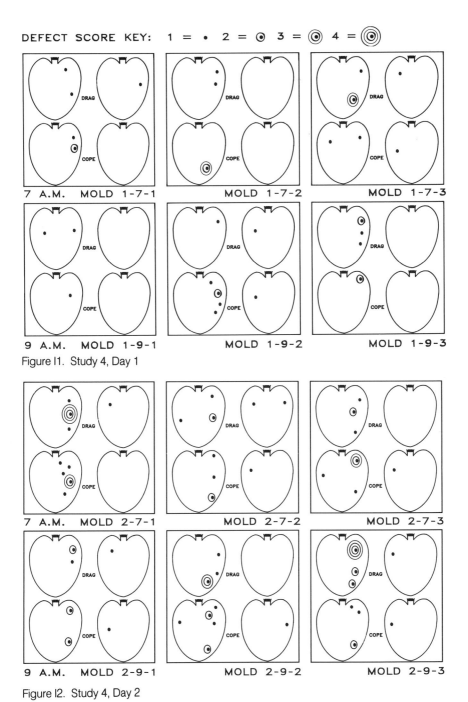

Figure I1. Study 4, Day 1

Figure I2. Study 4, Day 2

Figure I. Casting Porosity Study 4

Solutions

Study 1

Suppose the measles chart is divided into four sections by drawing diagonal lines through it as shown in Figure J. If the castings in study 1 were thus divided, the defect totals could be compared. There was four times as high a total defect score (96 to 24) on the section of the castings next to the gate (the upper part closer to the gate where the metal flows in) as there was in the rest of the sections of the castings further from the gate. An even larger difference can be seen between this portion nearest the gate and the left section; comparing these sections yields a ratio of 96 to 1. (The same procedure for division of the castings could be applied to the other studies.)

Figure J. Division of Casting

The causes of the 96 to 1 defect score ratio between the upper quarter of the castings (near the gate) and the left quarter of the castings might include the turbulence of the metal entering the gate trapping gases (possibly due to pouring too fast or to too much constriction in the gate area). Also, slag might be floating on the metal near the gate.

In another comparison, the total defect score in study 1 in the cope was twice as high as in the drag (80 to 40), a ratio of 2 to 1. With a 2 to 1 ratio of cope versus drag, perhaps trapped gases could not escape and were caught in the top half of the casting (cope); maybe better venting is needed. Or perhaps slag floating on the top of the metal caused more porosity in the cope.

Study 2

In study 2 the 7 a.m. defect score total was 73 and the 9 a.m. total was 35, just over a 2 to 1 ratio. The cope totaled 91 and the drag totaled 17, a ratio of almost 5.4 to 1.

The 7 a.m. scores might be twice as high as the 9 a.m. scores because of metal temperature, sand temperature and humidity, operator alertness, ambient temperature, daily startup problems, etc.; problems such as these might be overcome by 9 a.m. The 5.4 to 1 defect score ratio of cope to drag might be due to causes similar to those in study 1, i.e., trapped gases, floating slag, or the necessity for better venting.

Study 3

In study 3 the total defect score for 7 a.m. was 97 and at 9 a.m. 24, a ratio of about 4 to 1. The first day defect score totaled 80 and the second day totaled 41, a ratio of about 2 to 1. The 7 a.m. defect score might be four times as high as 9 a.m. for the same reasons as in study 2: problems encountered at 7 a.m. had been overcome by 9 a.m.

In contrast, the 2 to 1 defect score ratio of day 1 versus day 2 suggests other possibilities. Possibly day 1 was a Monday start up after a weekend shut down with its associated weekly start-up problems; possibly different crews, metallurgical differences, metal temperature, sand temperature and humidity, ambient temperature and humidity, crew alertness the first day of the week, etc., affected the results.

Study 4

In study 4, day 1 had a defect score of 35 and day 2 had a defect score of 71 for a ratio of about 1 to 2. Also, the left castings (including cope and drag) had a score of 91 while the right castings (cope and drag) had a score of 15, a ratio of over 6 to 1.

If the left side of all castings is compared to the right side of all castings, there is a difference of about 5.2 to 1; the right side total is 89 and the left side total is 17. This result is influenced by the 6 to 1 ratio between the left and right castings in the mold (91 to 15). However, if the observer adds the left side of the left castings to the right side of the right castings, he will obtain a total of 8 for the "outside half" of the two castings. If he adds the right side of the left castings to the left side of the right castings, he will get a total of 98 for the "inside half" of the two castings. Thus, there is a ratio of over 12 to 1 comparing the "inside" versus the "outside." This large ratio could easily be missed, partly because the 6 to 1 defect score ratio of the left casting versus the right casting tends to overshadow or mask this big difference. The comparison of "inside" versus "outside" is practical because the "inside" is more likely to retain heat, as a result of the castings being next to each other. The "outside" half could cool much more quickly, and the resulting temperature differential could cause defects.

Causes of the 6 to 1 defect score ratio from the left casting to the right casting could be attributed to pattern design and construction, because these two castings are supposed to be identical; they have the same sand, same metal, same crew, so forth. Causes of the 1 to 2 ratio of day 1 to day 2 might be somewhat similar to the possible causes in study 3 of the 2 to 1 ratio from day 1 to day 2 except that because day 2 is higher, the possible causes are not related to start up, but rather to the differences between one day and the next.

Further Study

It is appropriate to analyze these four multi-vari studies completely only by adding the totals as we have already done. The investigator could, however, plot the results. For instance, in Figure K the total defect scores (cope and drag combined) for the castings in study 3 are shown on a multi-vari chart. The day 1, 7 a.m., mold 1 castings have defect scores of 10 (left casting) and 12 (right casting). These two defect scores are plotted and are connected by a vertical line. In mold 2 the left casting totals 10 and the right casting totals 11; these two defect scores are plotted and connected to represent the score in the second mold. Similarly, the defect scores in mold 3 of 11 and 10 are plotted and connected. The mold 1, mold 2, and mold 3 averages are connected to represent the results at 7 a.m. on day 1.

A similar plot is made for the 9 a.m. results for day 1 and then the 7 a.m. and 9 a.m. results are plotted for day 2. All of these four sets of plots are captioned at the top of the figure. Then all the 7 a.m. results (day 1, 7 a.m. and day 2, 7 a.m.) are averaged, plotted with a dot halfway between the two sets of 7 a.m. plots, and labeled *7 a.m. Avg.* Also, the 9 a.m. results (for both days) are averaged, plotted with a dot halfway between the two sets of plots and labeled *9 a.m. Avg.* A dotted line between these two dots shows the 7 a.m. to 9 a.m. difference.

Similarly, the day 1 results are averaged, plotted with a dot halfway between the two sets of day 1 plots and labeled *Day 1 Avg.* The same procedure is done with the day 2 plots and labeled *Day 2 Avg.* These two dots are connected with a dashed line to highlight the difference between the two days. The dotted line connecting the 7 a.m. average to the 9 a.m. average is much steeper than the dashed line connecting *Day 1 Avg.* to *Day 2 Avg.* because the 7 a.m. to 9 a.m.

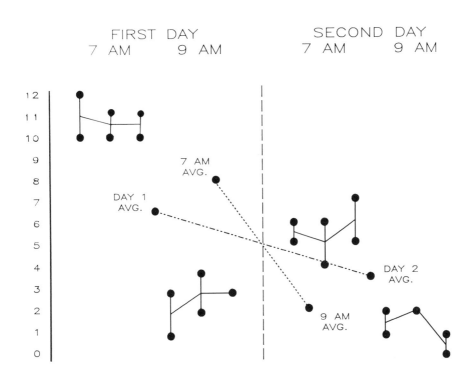

Figure K. Multi-Vari for Study 3 Data

defect score ratio was 4 to 1, while the day 1 to day 2 defect score ratio was 2 to 1.

These studies are not necessarily meant to be practical for detecting what causes porosity. The purpose is to give the reader an opportunity to practice the multi-vari approach and to determine patterns of variation that provide clues as to which variables may cause problems. These variables become prime candidates for other studies including a designed experiment, often the next step in the key variable isolation problem-solving strategy.

Glossary

The definitions of words and terms in this glossary are not intended to set standards for usage but to clarify the meaning of the word or term as it is used in this book.

Analysis of Variance (ANOVA) — a statistical procedure used for analyzing designed experiments. ANOVA compares mean square variation due to variables and interactions (the signal) to mean square variation due to residual error (noise). The purpose of ANOVA is to see if the variation in the experiment attributable to the variables and/or interactions is large enough to stand out above the variation in the residual, i.e., variation not explainable by the variables and interactions under investigation. The statistical mathematical procedure for performing ANOVA is complex but software is available to do the calculations. The theory and procedure of ANOVA are presented in numerous texts on statistical analysis and designed experiments, such as Dixon, Wilfrid J. and Massey, Frank J. Jr., *Introduction to Statistical Analysis* (New York: McGraw-Hill Book Company, Inc., 1957).

Attributes — product characteristics that are visual, workmanship or cosmetic rather than dimensional in nature. Attributes are usually designated as "good" or "bad," "acceptable" or "unacceptable," "satisfactory" or "unsatisfactory." In the key variable isolation strategy, attributes are always quantified by applying a numerical scale to them.

Capping Run — a production run made after various testing is completed to verify that the conclusions drawn are correct.

Clock Diagram — a graphic representation of an object or condition plotted as though it were on the face of a clock. The roundness and surface condition of circular or cylindrical objects such as crankshaft journals and patterns such as the wavefront propagation from an antenna are often plotted on clock diagrams or similar graphs. Measurements are made at numerous locations and are plotted on the diagram. A zero reference line (or point) is plotted on the diagram and deviations, plus or minus, of out of plane, out of round or eccentricity are plotted around the "clock" face. If out of round were being plotted and there was no measurable out of round, the plot would show all points on the zero reference line. The clock diagram provides a graphic picture of the amount and direction of the deviation from a perfect product or condition.

Component Search — a testing technique that uses an assembly which is functioning very well and an assembly that is functioning very badly. These assemblies are first tested separately and the results recorded. Then, the component search process is started by exchanging parts (components) between the two assemblies. The first component exchanged is the one that is believed to be the most likely cause of the difference in performance. The two assemblies with the exchanged components are then tested again. This exchange of components can produce a variety of results, such as:

1. The results of the testing after the component was exchanged are about the same as they were before the component was exchanged, suggesting that the suspected component is not the cause of the problem (i.e., not the key variable).

2. The results are about the same as those from the previous testing except the results are reversed. That is, when the most suspect component was changed, the results changed with it. This means that the first component chosen for exchange is the cause of the difference in performance.

3. The results are somewhere between the above two results, that is, the better assembly became somewhat degraded and the poorer assembly became somewhat better. These results indicate that the first component chosen is important but that there are other important ones as well. The degree by which the results fall between the two results above indicates the relative importance of the most suspect component. If one set of results changes but not the other, or both get better or both get worse, this indicates an interaction in which the effect of one component depends on which assembly it is in.

In component search, the first few exchanges are made one component at a time. However, after these exchanges are made, several components may be exchanged at the same time to speed up the process. The process of exchanging components continues until all the important exchanges have been made, i.e., the original test result differences between the two assemblies have been switched from one assembly to the other. Then the industrial investigator returns to the original configuration of components and repeats the test to see if the original test results are obtained. The purpose of returning to the original configuration is to ensure that other unknown factors have not changed during the time the tests were run.

The analysis of a component search procedure is generally done by plotting the data rather than by elaborate calculations.

Fast-Shot Length — in aluminum die casting, the injection cycle consists of a slow phase, an acceleration phase and a fast phase. The fast-shot length is the distance the plunger travels during the fast phase as it injects molten aluminum into the die cavity.

Fast-Shot Velocity — in aluminum die casting, the injection cycle consists of a slow phase, an acceleration phase and a fast phase. The fast-shot velocity is the speed at which the plunger travels during the fast phase as it injects molten aluminum into the die cavity.

Flash — an overfilled condition which results in thin excess plastic attached to a molded plastic product at die lines, parting lines and knock-out pin bosses.

Fractional Factorial Designed Experiment — an experiment in which only a carefully selected number of all the levels of variables are tested. Fewer tests are required than with full factorial experiments, resulting in the loss of some information about potential interactions.

Framing or Bracketing — the process of identifying the types or classes of variables that are causing the greatest variation.

Full Factorial Designed Experiment — an experiment in which every combination of all levels of all variables is tested.

Industrial Investigator — a person or team that applies the tools, techniques and strategies of key variable isolation to learn which variables or interactions are at the root of a product problem.

Isoplot — a graph on which the X (horizontal) scale represents the readings of one inspector or instrument and the Y (vertical) scale represents the readings of a second inspector or instrument. An isoplot is used to graphically represent the agreement of these two sets of readings. For example, if the first inspector obtained exactly the same reading as the second inspector on all units being measured, the points would all be plotted on the 45-degree line of perfect agreement. Points not on the 45-degree line indicate disagreement between readings.

Median Chart — a median chart is an alternative to the average or X-bar chart. On a median chart the middle, or median, number or value is plotted, thus eliminating the need to calculate the average. For example, if 4, 5 and 8 are measurements made on three parts, the average or 5.7 would be plotted on an X-bar chart, and the median number, or 5, would be plotted on a median chart. The median chart control limits are calculated differently from X-bar chart control limits. A median chart is less subject to being greatly influenced by one number that is considerably higher or lower than the other numbers in the sample. See Grant, Eugene L. and Leavenworth, Richard S., *Statistical Quality Control* (New York: McGraw-Hill Book Company, Inc., 1987).

Multiple Balance — a form of fractional factorial experiment in which a small number of all variables at all levels are tested. Multiple balance is similar to random balance; however, within the overall test design, one or more full factorial experiments are run together while the levels of all the other variables are chosen randomly. The analysis of a multiple balance test is done in total as in a random balance test, but the full factorial formats within the experiment are analyzed separately as any other full factorial experiment would be. Multiple balance is often considered a screening test because there is the potential for missing some interactions. (See also Random Balance).

Numerical Scale — the numbers assigned to varying levels of quality for a product characteristic that is visual, workmanship or cosmetic. Developing a numerical scale is a prerequisite for running a multi-vari study. A numerical scale can also be a tool for judging the effect of process changes, for monitoring quality trends of a process and for auditing the output of a process.

Open-Ended Questions — in this book, open-ended questions are contrasted to closed-ended questions. A closed-ended question might be, "Is temperature the key variable?" An open-ended question might be, "Does the pattern of variation indicate that the key variable causes variation within the piece, piece to piece, time to time or machine to machine, etc.?" The answer to an open-ended question is usually a type or class of variables that tends to rule out those variables which have a pattern of variation that does not agree with the observed pattern of variation.

Percent Defective — the portion of manufactured products that is determined not to meet specifications. If, for example, 200 products are made and 30 of these are defective, the production run would be 15 percent defective.

Piece-to-Piece Variation — variation from one piece to the next piece. Piece-to-piece variation analysis is typically performed on consecutive pieces as they come from a machine or production line. Piece-to-piece variation often suggests random variation in the operation, variation introduced from earlier processes and/or measurement error. The evidence of excessive piece-to-piece variation usually rules out process variables such as temperature, raw material, etc., because these variables are unlikely to change between the production of consecutive pieces.

Process Latitude Study — a study done to determine the

tolerances (or latitude) which are appropriate for process input variables. The study is run by setting process input variables at the limits of the current specification and testing to see what effect these settings have on the process output. For example, if the process latitude study shows that operating with a process input variable, such as temperature, set at its high limit creates too much variation in a product dimension, such as length, then the operating tolerance limits for temperature must be reduced. Conversely, if varying the process input variable from the maximum to the minimum tolerance has no measurable effect on the output, then the tolerance can be opened up and retested to set new, wider tolerance limits.

Pull Test — a tensile test in which a specified force is applied to a feature such as a welded or soldered joint or to the lead of an electronic component. The joint or component is then tested to see if it still meets the requirements.

Random Balance — a form of fractional factorial experiment in which only a small fraction of the total number of combinations of all variables at all levels is tested. The selection of which combination of variables is tested at which levels is done more or less randomly. Balance is achieved by performing the same number of tests at each variable condition. As with any fractionalized experiment, the opportunity to evaluate some interactions is lost. However, less rigidity in planning and execution is required compared to classical fractional factorials. Random balance is most effective as a screening test which looks for the major factors influencing variation.

Random Number Table — a set of randomly selected numbers in which each number has an equal and independent chance to be selected. Random numbers are used to design tests or experiments so as to reduce or eliminate the effects of shifts, trends, cyclical variation or other forms of bias during sampling or test evaluation. See Dixon, Wilfrid J. and Massey, Frank J. Jr., *Introduction to Statistical Analysis* (New York: McGraw-Hill Book Company, Inc., 1957.)

Repeat — a process operation that is performed more than once without changing process input settings or conditions.

Replication — a test condition in which process input variables are set to levels different from a previous run, the process is run with the new settings, then the settings are reset to the original settings and the process is rerun. A replicate is different from a repeat. A replicate only occurs if other combinations of variables are run and then the process is reset to the original combination of variables to run the subsequent replicate. (Compare with *Repeat.*)

Short Shot — a condition caused by injecting an insufficient amount of plastic into a mold cavity, resulting in an incompletely molded part. (The term *short shot* is also used in die casting and molten metal injection.)

Splay — an elongated, silvery surface imperfection on a molded plastic product which sometimes appears as an unusually high gloss area or minor delamination. Splay is usually caused by volatiles (moisture, monomer, degradation products, etc.) in the melt stream in the form of bubbles which fracture at the surface of the cavity during the injection phase of the cycle.

Stratified Sampling — the selection of samples from a process based on a plan that provides the most likelihood of showing variation from piece to piece, time to time, shift to shift, machine to machine, etc. (Within-piece variation can be determined from either stratified or random sampling.) A stratified sample provides the most information on patterns of variation with the smallest number of samples. A random sample, on the other hand, is intended to give an unbiased indication of quality on an already produced lot of products often for the purpose of deciding to accept or reject the lot of material.

Time-to-Time Variation — variation in a product from one time period to another time period, either short term or longer term.

Type or Class of Variables — that portion of the entire list of process input variables that causes common patterns of variation. For example, if the greatest variation is from first shift to second shift, then the type or class of variables for further investigation would only include those variables that can vary from first shift to second shift.

Variables — process parameters such as temperature, pressure, time, speed, etc. This usage should not be confused with variables inspection, which refers to using measured product characteristics. It is generally accepted that process variables can vary within limits without causing excessive variation in the product made by the process. When a process variable varies excessively, or, if it is set to an inappropriate level (e.g., temperature set too high), that condition causes the product to be defective. The process variable is then referred to as a *key* variable.

Variables Search — a technique by which the levels or settings of process variables are exchanged between "good" and "bad" levels. Variables search is similar to component search except that settings of process variables, rather than components, are exchanged.

Variation — the difference in quality, performance or measurement between two or more products or conditions. The difference in the weights of two packages of frozen food, for example, would be called the variation in weight. Variation can occur in one of two categories: acceptable variation (i.e., variation within or less than specified limits) or excessive variation. Excessive variation is considered symptomatic of process problems caused by one or more key process variables.

Void — an internal imperfection in a molded plastic product, which resembles a bubble but contains a near vacuum instead of being pressurized. A void is usually the result of phase shrinkage (transition from a fluid phase to a solid phase) and thermal shrinkage during the cooling phase of the cycle. Typically, a void is found in thick-walled areas which, during cooling, form rigid skins capable of supporting the negative internal pressure that develops as the liquid center continues to cool.

Within-Piece Variation — variation that exists in the dimension or physical appearance of the same feature of the same part or piece, i.e., from end to end, side to side, top to bottom, etc. Excessive within-piece variation, such as out of round, taper, location of air entrapment, foreign material location, deformed shape, etc., often is caused by peculiarities of the manufacturing equipment or process such as misalignment, inadequate venting, poor die design, etc. Evidence of within-piece variation rules out many process variables that could not change within one piece.

Index

Acceptance plan, product 92
Analysis of variance 67, 121
Analyzer, sound spectrum 73-74
Anechoic chamber 73
ANOVA (see analysis of variance)
Approach, traditional engineering 2, 16, 45, 87, 125
Attributes 10, 39, 94, 106
Audit, quality 24
Balanced experiments 38-39
Bias 128, 134
Bimodal distribution 101-102
Brainstorming 119-121
Brown, Gregory 87
Capping run(s) 120
Case history 4
Casting, aluminum die (see die casting, aluminum)
Cavities 43-44,46-49
Cells 65
Characteristic, defect 10, 42, 46-49, 56, 90, 94, 130
Cleaner, ultrasonic 92
Clock diagram 95-96
Clue(s) 5, 8-9, 32, 37, 44, 68, 74-75, 77, 96, 119
Complaints, customer 70
Component search 108-110, 124
Concentricity 74-77
Confounded results 23, 73
Consensus 13, 134
Continuous improvement 94
Control limits 94
Correlation 74, 128
Covers, tamperproof 46
Cryptography 79
Cylinder liners 56
Decibel 75
Defect (see characteristic)
Defect scores (see quantification)
Defective, definition of 1, 125-126
Designed experiment (see experiment, designed)
Dial indicator 35, 92-93, 95
Die casting, aluminum 87-88, 90-91, 95, 97
Diminishing returns, point of 81, 113
Error, residual 26-27, 82, 86
Experiment, designed or factorial 9, 19, 20, 25-28, 32-33, 37-39, 53-56, 64-69, 79-86, 88, 103, 110-115, 118-121, 125-126
Experiment, fractional factorial 48, 82, 121
Experts, panel of 13
Factor(s) (see variable(s))

Factorial designed experiments (see experiment, designed or factorial)
Fan 31-33
Fast-shot length 88-90
Fast-shot velocity 88-90
Forming, cold 35, 37, 40
Fractional factorial experiment (see experiment, fractional factorial)
Frame or bracket 3
Head
  filling, sealing, 21-24
  winding, 15-16
Hot crank 105-114
Industrial detective work 3
Industrial investigator (see investigator, industrial)
Injection molding (see molding, injection)
Inspection, incoming quality control 98
Interaction 17-19, 23, 25-26, 37-38, 43, 60-62, 67-69, 73, 103
Internship 4
Investigator, industrial 2-3, 5, 27, 97
Isoplot 72-73, 127-134
Job shop 94
Kelvin, Lord 10-11
Key variable(s), [key process variable(s)] [see variable(s), key]
Key variable isolation 2-3, 5, 45, 55, 63, 87, 92, 96-97, 124
Leakers (leaks) 20-24, 63-68
Leason, Art 70
Levels of testing 25, 37, 47-48, 58, 64, 82-84, 88, 117-122, 124-126
Loss function 94
Machines, forming 46
Main effects 61, 88
Maldistribution theory (see Pareto)
Management task force [see team(s), problem solving]
Measles chart 30, 43, 64, 88-90
Median 84
Median chart 40
Methods, traditional engineering (see approach, traditional engineering)
Metrology 75
Mold 43-44
Molding,injection 42, 44, 118
Multiple balance 86
Multi-vari studies 2, 5-9, 14-16, 25, 30, 35-37, 42-43, 46-47, 56-58, 63-64, 71-73, 77, 91-93, 95, 101-103, 117-119
Myths 33
Noise (see error, residual)
Nonparallel response (see interaction)

Normal curve 101
Numerical rating scale (see quantification)
Open-ended question 3
Optimum 88-90
Overstress testing (see testing, overstress)
Oxide stringer 20-24
Parallel path experimentation 124-126
Pareto 42-43, 63, 79-81, 112
Pass testing 100
Patterns of variation (see variation,
    patterns of)
Plunger, misaligned 38-41
Point of diminishing returns (see
    diminishing returns, point of)
Pollard, John 78
Porosity 29, 33-34, 88-90
Pre-control 93-94
Problem-solving team(s) [see team(s),
    problem solving]
Process control 92
Process latitude study (see study, process
    latitude)
Pull test (see test, pull)
Quantification 10-12,21, 29-31, 42, 45, 47,
    56-60, 71, 88, 90-92, 100, 106-108,
    120, 130
Random balance 78
Random number table 32, 39, 53
Randomization 21, 23, 32, 37, 39, 46, 58-59,
    65-66, 84-86, 88, 117
Rath & Strong, Inc. iii
Reddy, John M. 20, 78
Reddy, Rosen, Traver & Woods, Inc., iv
Remedy, "Old Timers" 29
Repeat(s) 59, 117-119
Repeatability 39, 73, 93, 107-108, 114, 117
Replicate(s) 26, 39, 59, 65, 83-84, 120
Reproducibility 73
Residual error (see error, residual)
Rosen, Charles L. 98
Rough screening (see screening, rough)
Safety margin 68
Sampling 90
Sampling, stratified 5, 9, 58, 79, 84
Sampling theory 79-81
Satterthwaite, Dr. Frank 79-81
Scale, numerical rating (see quantification)
Scale, variable (see quantification)
Scatter plots 84-86
Scores, defect (see quantification)
Screening, rough 81-86, 117, 121
Setup plan 94
Shainin, Dorian iii, 117
Shewhart, Walter iv
Shorts 42
Signal 27
Sound spectrum analyzer (see analyzer,
    sound spectrum)
Splay 118-121
Startability 108-115
Station, filling/sealing 20-22

Statistical process control (SPC) 87, 96
Stratified sampling (see sampling,
    stratified)
Study, process latitude 47
Task force [see team(s), problem solving]
Team(s), problem solving 11, 20-24, 29, 46,
    48, 56-58, 63, 70-71, 78, 87, 100,
    105-114, 118-122, 126
Test, pull 122
Testing, overstress, 63-64
Thickness, wall 35, 37, 39
Tolerance analysis study (see study, process
    latitude)
Total indicator reading (TIR) 75
Traditional engineering approach (see
    approach, traditional engineering)
"Traffic light" 94
Transformers 14
Trivial many 81-82
Twenty questions 8-9, 126
Ultrasonic cleaner (see cleaner, ultrasonic)
United States Pharmacopoeia (USP) 98
Variable(s), key 1, 5, 9, 21, 25, 37, 44-45,
    47-48, 58, 61, 64, 72-73, 81-85, 103,
    110-115, 117-123, 126
Variable scale(s) (see quantification)
Variables search 117-123, 124
Variation, patterns of 2, 5, 31-32, 48, 64, 87,
    92, 96
    cavity-to-cavity 47
    coil-to-coil 15
    cycle-to-cycle 64
    engine-to-engine 115
    head-to-head 22
    heat-to-heat 42-44
    lot-to-lot 95
    machine-to-machine 36, 57-58
    operator-to-operator 57-58
    out-of-plane 95-96
    piece-to-piece (unit-to-unit) 6
    place-to-place 102
    ring-to-ring 30
    run-to-run 118
    shift-to-shift 5
    shot-to-shot 42
    station-to-station 22
    time-to-time 6
    within a shift 91
    within-batch 102
    within-mold 42-43
    within-piece (within unit) 6, 8
    within-ring 30
    in aluminum die castings 91
    in artillery projectiles 35-37
    in castings 57-59
    in cleaning 91
    in compression molding 46-47
    in decorative rings 30
    in dust cover seals 42-44
    in machining 93
    in noisy motors 71

166   Traver